COOK WITH MATCHA & GREEN TEA

ULTIMATE GUIDE & RECIPES FOR BREWING AND COOKING WITH MATCHA & GREEN TEA

DEDICATION

TO   MY LOVELY WIFE MIKI

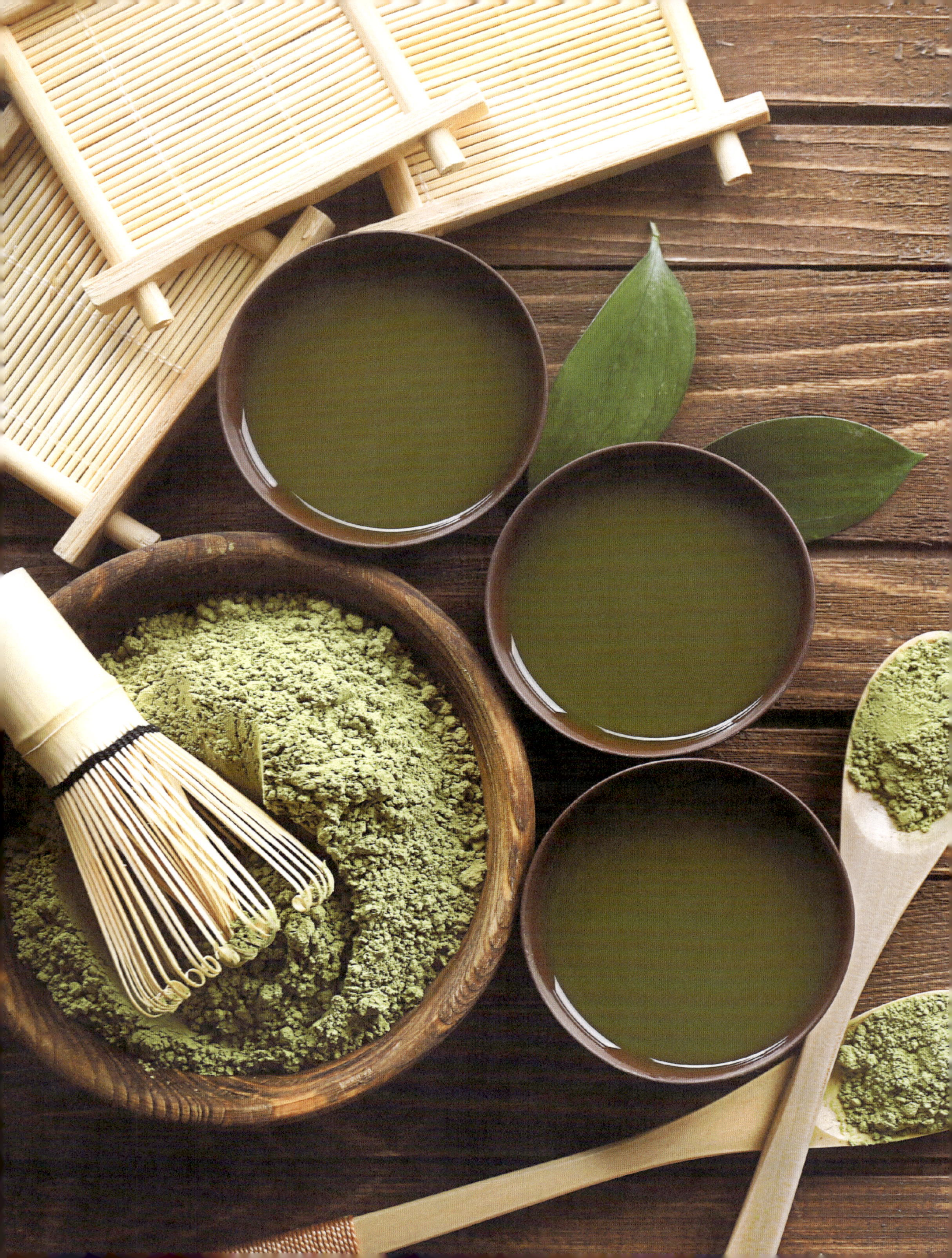

Table of Contents

Section 1

THE BASIC – MAKING YOUR TEA TASTES BETTER

Section 2

INTERMEDIATE – VARIETY OF GREEN TEA DRINKS

Section 3

THE ADVANCED - COOK WITH GREEN TEA

ACKNOWLEDGMENTS

I would like to thank Mr. Jurgen Link and Mr. Wesley Dameron for mentoring through SCORE and guiding me to navigate through crowded world.

6

-INTRODUCTION-

Since I started Japanese Green Tea Company, I have had occasions where I get to interact with many tea specialists and tea lovers.

In such occasions, often times, I have been asked for recommendations of recipe book using matcha and green tea.

There are many books out there which explain traditional tea and tea ceremonies, but often, people are simply looking for a way to enjoy matcha at home on their own kitchen.

My goal of this book was simple.

I WANTED TO CREATE A RECIPE BOOK SO THAT EVERY AMERICAN CAN ENJOY GREEN TEA & MATCHA AT HOME.

I decided to segment this book into three sections:

1. Basics of how to brew Japanese green tea

2. The variety of modern green tea drinks such as smoothies and cocktail recipes.

3. Cooking with green tea, including recipe such as green tea bread, sweets, and cakes

I collaborated with professional chefs and tea industry experts to make this book available so that everyone can enjoy Japanese tea in the 21st century American home.
Japanese green tea is one of the healthiest beverages in the world.

I hope you get to enjoy these great recipes in the comfort of your own home and become healthy at the same time.

KEI NISHIDA
Author, CEO, Japanese Green Tea Company

SECTION 1

THE BASIC MAKING YOUR TEA TASTES BETTER

01 How to Brew Tasty Japanese Green Tea

Japanese green tea can be brewed in different ways. In this chapter, we will go over the Simple way and the Advanced Way for brewing tasty green tea. The Simple way is how most Japanese consume green tea every day; the Advanced Way is what is being followed by professional green tea producers who recommend the best approach for brewing the most tasty Japanese green tea.

We recommend that you start with the Simple way to enjoy the approcch for the Advance Way. After trying out simple ways to appreciate the difference in taste and aroma that it brings.

HOW TO BREW TASTY JAPANESE GREEN TEA

No special equipment like a teapot is needed for this method. You can use any mesh strainer to filter the green tea.

1. Dissolve two teaspoons of powder into 8 Oz of hot water. We recommend about 175°F for most common green tea.

2. Wait for 60-120 seconds

3. Filter out the green tea leaves using a mesh strainer and serve hot.

1. SELECTING THE RIGHT TEAPOT

This approach requires a Japanese Teapot. There are different types of teapots, but for our green tea which is deep steamed green tea (Fukamushi-cha), we recommend Fukamushi teapot which is explicitly made for Deep Steam Green Tea. Fukamushi tea containing finer leaves since it qualifies what exactly deep steam tea is. Characteristic of Fukamushi teapot is that it has a more beautiful mesh to be able to capture finer tea leaves as tea leaves.

The picture shown is 12Oz Fukamushi Teapot.

If you do not have access to Fukamushi Teapot, you can use any type of teapots, but try to find ones with finer mesh when brewing Fukamushi.

2. SELECTING AND BOILING WATER THE RIGHT WAY

Water is essential when brewing green tea. It is best to use soft water with less mineral to get the best result. Hard water with mineral breaks down elements in green tea which breaks the taste.

If you have any access to water softer filtering system, use them. If using bottled water, do not use the ones with "Added Mineral." Evian tends to be recommended ones as they are known for soft water.

Boil water until 212°F for 4-5 minutes and cool down to 175°F. By boiling water first, it removes the smell of chloride. This approach in Japanese is called "yuzamashi" which translates to "cooled-down" water.

3. PUT GREEN TEA

Add a spoon of deep-steamed green tea leaves into the teapot. (1-2 teaspoon is good for 2~3 people, approximately one teaspoon is good for one person)

Please add the number of tea leaves according to your favor and the teapot in use.

4.   PUT HOT WATER

Turn some cooled boiled water (8-10 Oz) into the teapot.

The trick is to fill the teapot with 70% hot water. By doing so, it spreads the scent to the remaining 30 percent of the teapot.

5.   ROTATE TEAPOT

Rotate the teapot slowly for about 60 seconds. This allows green tea to open up and soak hot water evenly.

6. POUR GREEN TEA TO CUP

When pouring green tea into many teacups, do not pour one after the other (cup 1-> cup 2-> cup 3). By doing so, green tea in cup1 is lighter than cup 3 since the darker element of green tea tends to sit at the bottom of the tea..

Pour little by little by rotating each cup. (cup 1->cup 2-> cup 3-> cup 1-> cup 2-> cup 3). For 370cc teapot in the cup, rotate about 3-4 times between cups. Pouring using this method enables each cup to taste the same.

7.   POUR UNTIL THE LAST DROP

Pour to the last drop.The bottom drops of the teapot tend to be darker in color. The last drops have the most amount of aroma and elements, so you do not want tc miss out on the best part

8. ENJOY!

Hope you enjoy mellowsweet, and tasty Japanese Green Tea poured withserved in the traditional Japanese way.

02 How to Cold Brew Japanese Green Tea

If you're a tea lover, why not try cold brewing your next pot of Japanese green tea? Cold brewing might sound complicated if you haven't tried it before, but it's actually a simple process that results in a uniquely sweet, smooth tea. Cold brewing also offers several unique health benefits that you won't get if you brew your tea with hot water. Keep reading to learn about the process of cold brewing Japanese green tea.

What Makes Cold Brewing Different?

As the name implies, cold brewing means the tea is brewed with cold water instead of hot water. One of the main differences between cold and hot brewing is that cold brewing takes quite a bit longer. While a cup of hot tea is ready to drink within five minutes, cold brewed tea must steep for at several hours While this long brewing time can be annoying if you want to drink your tea right away, you can get around the wait by making a large pot of cold brewed tea before you go to bed and letting it steep overnight. You'll be able to sip on the finished product throughout the next day.

Even though it takes longer to make cold brewed tea, it's worth the wait. Tea brewed without any heat tastes different from traditional hot tea – it's sweeter, smoother, and doesn't have any of the bitter notes that you can sometimes taste in a cup of hot tea. This is because cold water doesn't extract tannins, the chemical responsible for that astringent(means geeky tea/wine term)taste, from the tea leaves. If you like to add sugar to your tea, you might be pleasantly surprised to find that cold brewed tea is already sweet enough on its own. Cold brewed Japanese green tea also offers a couple of distinct health benefits. First, it contains less caffeine than tea brewed with hot water, which is good news if you're trying to avoid the jitters. Cold water doesn't extract much caffeine from the leaves, so you can go ahead and drink a cup of cold-brewed green tea before bed because– it won't keep you awake.

Second, cold brewed green tea contains more antioxidants than hot tea. According to a video posted by Dr. Michael Greger at NutritionFacts.org, a team of Italian researchers discovered that hot water destroys some of the catechins – the chemicals with antioxidant properties – in tea leaves. Conversely, cold water extracts those catechins without harming them. While any type of green tea is good for you, you'll get more of its disease-fighting and anti-aging properties by choosing the cold brewed variety.

Cold Brewing

Method 1: Using Cool Water

This method of cold brewing takes a while to steep - a minimum of three hours is recommended. However, the advantage of this method is that it works well for any grade of green tea. In fact, even cheaper green teas usually taste excellent when they're brewed with cool water.

To make tea with this method, use a ratio of one to two tablespoons of tea leaves per quart of water. For a quick and convenient alternative, you can also use regular green tea bags. Place the tea leaves in the bottom of a large container or kyusu (A kyusu is a traditional Japanese teapot mainly used for brewing green teat). Then, add the water, cover the container, and place it in the refrigerator to steep. When you're ready, give the finished pot a gentle swirl or a stir before you drink it since the

stronger-flavored sediment may settle at the bottom during brewing.

My favorite way is to use a tea filter bag and loose leaf green tea. Usually higher grade green tea is available in loose leaf form and not tea bag form.

Here is a link to an amazon to get one of these tea filter bags:
https://www.amazon.com/gp/product/BC0QQF4XT2/ref=as_li_tl?ie=UTF8&camp=1789&creative=9325&creativeASIN=B00QQF4XT2&linkCode=as2&tag=greentea08b-20&linkId=17a5c7e80b33fac9a4f1b4f3cae86649

You can simply put green tea in disposable tea filter bag and close the lid on filter.

Put in one litre jar

Add water (filtered water is recommended).

After letting it sit for 3 - 24 hours, stir well before drinking.,

To get the most out of your tea leaves, you should let the tea sit in the refrigerator for at least three hours. However, you can let it steep for up to twenty-four hours for a stronger brew if you want. Unlike hot tea, cold brewed tea won't get bitter the longer you steep it. Therefore, many people like to let their tea steep overnight with this method so they can drink it in the morning.

Cold Brewing Method 2: Using Ice

This is another simple way to make cold brewed tea. The advantage of this method is that it produces a tea with a very light, delicate taste. This steeping method works best for high-quality teas that are naturally flavorful; so, you may want to use a good loose-leaf tea instead of a regular tea bag.

To make cold brewed green tea with ice, place one to two tablespoons of loose tea leaves in your pot or kyusu. Then, fill the pot the rest of the way with ice and let it sit undisturbed. When the ice has melted, your tea will be ready to drink. If you aren't using a kyusu, strain the leaves through a mesh sieve or cheesecloth before you serve the tea.

24

Cold Brewing Method 3: Cooling Hot Tea

Cold brewing can be a lengthy process. But, if you're impatient to drink your tea, you can just brew a quick cup of hot green tea and then cool it with ice. This method works equally well with loose-leaf tea and tea bags. One thing to keep in mind, however, is that the ice will water down the tea, so, you may want to make your tea stronger than you normally would. Try doubling the amount of tea leaves you use or using two tea bags instead of one.

Notes on Cold Brewing

Don't throw out those tea leaves after you make a pot of cold brewed green tea. Most tea leaves can be used more than once, especially if you're not using hot water. Keep in mind, however, that your second pot of tea may have a lighter flavor than the first. If you are using a kyusu, it will filter the loose-leaf tea for you. If not, you can strain the tea through a cheesecloth or a fine mesh sieve to remove the leaves.

26

03 More Tips to Make Your Green Tea Tastier

Green tea, which is made from Camellia sinensis leaves, is widely known to have a wealth of health benefits. The tea originated in the country of China, before quickly spreading throughout the Asian continent. Today, people all around the globe consume the delicious drink as a way to improve their health, boost their immunity and enhance their brain functions. Nevertheless, many westerners do not understand the precious protocols involved with traditional green tea preparation. Most opt for the most convenient and quickest method. Are you positive you're getting the most from your green tea?

No Universal Procedure

There is often a misconception that there is a singular, universal procedure for properly preparing traditional Chinese and Japanese tea. This couldn't be further from the truth. The various preparation techniques are very diverse much like the people that enjoy the drink on a regular basis. Sen no Rikyu, who greatly influenced the traditional Japanese tea ceremony, often expressed the simplistic nature of preparing tea. He also placed great emphasis on honesty of one's self. The renowned tea master also concluded that proper preparation required nothing more than boiling the water, making the tea and enjoying.

Even with the Japanese "Way of Tea" ceremony, the chain of events tends to differ based on venue, season, time of the day, and other factors. With this in mind, it is best to rely on the wisdom of Sen no Rikyu. As long as you're true to yourself, there is no wrong way to prepare your green tea.

The Basic Protocol

For the people of China and Japan, brewing green tea is truly an art. For others, extravagance is not a necessity. Again, as Sen no Rikyu pointed out, simplicity is best. Despite the mythology associated with traditional tea ceremonies, the most common preparation methods are straightforward. First and foremost, grab the teapot or Kyusu. The teapot should be preheated with hot water. Pour out the water and add the tea leaves to the pot. Then, add hot water to the pot and wait it out. Give the tea enough time to take on a life of its own. Before long, that delicious aroma will fill your nostrils. After that, you can add the concoction to your tea cups and enjoy.

Choosing A TeaPot

There are many factors to consider when shopping for a new teapot. Clay is the most popular material utilized to create Chinese teapots, which says a lot about the quality of the material. The type of firing utilized during the production process is extremely

29

utilized to create the teapot. Purple clay is derived from Yixing a county-level city in the People's Republic of China and is the most popular among Chinese teapot manufacturers.

High-fired teapots constructed from thin clay are perfect for everyday tea use and a necessity for white, oolong and green teas. Low-fired teapots are more suitable for Pu-erh and black tea or red tea because they are constructed from a more porous and thicker clay.

Source of Water

If you are an avid tea drinker, you probably understand the importance of water. When selecting a specific type of water for tea, you must consider that water is not manmade, but in fact, something that Mother Nature provides. However, some manufacturers produce different types of waters, such as sterile water, spring water, drinking water and distilled water, while others are created right in the comfort of one's home. The processes that are most often utilized to create artificial water are reverse osmosis, filtration, and boiling.

The beauty of water is that it can en

hance the flavors of the tea, depending on where it comes from and how it is produced. To get the most out of your tap water, if this is the water source you prefer, is to filter out the impurities before adding it to the tea. You can do this by utilizing a fine strainer or store bought filter. Just flush the water through the filter to remove all of the impurities, which can produce a foul odor and taste. The end result will be a delicious cup of tea, with flavors that will roll off your tongue. If you do not have access to a filter, you can boil the water to remove the bacteria, which takes about 20 minutes on the maximum temperature level. The key is to eliminate the elements that are responsible for altering the flavors, effects and aromas of the tea.

Water Temperature Is Paramount

After you've acquired the best water, it is time to get started. Temperature will play a paramount role in determining the aroma and flavor that you're able to achieve. Nevertheless, your own personal often utilized to create artificial water are reverse osmosis, filtration, and boiling. The beauty of water is that it can enhance the flavors of the tea, depending on where it comes from and how it is produced. To get the most out of your tap water, if this is the water source you prefer, is to filter out the impurities before adding it to the tea. You can do this by utilizing a fine strainer or store bought filter. Just flush the water through the filter to remove all of the impurities, which can produce a foul odor and taste. The end result will be a delicious cup of tea, with flavors that will roll off your tongue.

If you do not have access to a filter, you can boil the water to remove the bacteria, which takes about 20 minutes on the maximum temperature level. The key is to eliminate the elements that are responsible for altering the flavors, effects and aromas of the tea.

Water Temperature Is Paramount

After you've acquired the best water, it is time to get started. Temperature will play a paramount role in determining the aroma and flavor that you're able to achieve. Nevertheless, your own personal preferences should not be ignored. The temperature selected will alter the potency and boldness of the tea. Preparing the tea at a lower temperature helps to prolong its flavor. Alternatively, a higher temperature can help to extract the tea's scrumptious aroma with greater effect. Many consumers will prefer to find a balance between aroma, flavor, and astringency. This is why Sencha is so incredibly popular in the country of Japan. When prepared at a temperature of 70-degrees Celsius, Sencha will deliver a pleasant flavor, while the bitterness will be minimized. Increasing the temperature to 90-degrees Celsius can provide a better balance, while simultaneously promoting a strong aroma.

In order to truly find that sweet spot, it is pertinent to experiment extensively with different preparation methods and different varieties of tea.

Different Teas

Learning how to masterfully prepare your green tea can be very complicated, due to the sheer number of

Anyone who has watched an episode of America's Test Kitchen understands how the insights of food science can improve the flavors of our favorite dishes. Green tea is no exception. It has been the subject of countless scientific studies focused on flavor. The following ten tips, gleaned from this research, guarantee your next cup of green tea will be unforgettably delicious.

1. origin/terrior affects flavor

Flavor is subjective. To say that green tea from a particular region is better than green tea from another region supposes that we all have the same palate. Summarizing several studies, Alice Chi Phung identified different flavors of green tea associated with variants from different growing regions. African green teas have a "green, floral, fruity and nutty aroma." Indian and South Asian green teas were found to have a "green, floral, woody and citrus aroma." Northeast Asian teas had a "green and floral aroma." Green tea from Japan is part cularly sought out for its sweet, mellow flavor. Choose your favorite based on your personal preference.

2. Making the Grade

How and when green tea is harvested heavily influences its quality. The most flavorful green teas are harvested by hand in the spring. Only the most recent leaves, traditionally the two leaves at the tip of the new shoot, are harvested. The finest grades of Japanese green teas are deprived of light for weeks before the harvest. This technique forces the plant to produce excess chlorophyll and amino acids, and results in a sweeter tea. Stick with the higher end green teas, and stay away from bagged green teas, if you want to experience the amazing flavor of this first harvest. Japanese Green Tea offers Premium grade teas that are traditionally harvested.

3. Limited Oxidation = Unlimited Flavor

The Camellia sinensis plant produces all true teas. The difference in flavor and chemical composition comes from the amount of oxidation, or exposure to the air, that the plucked leaves undergo. Green tea leaves are heated soon after harvest to halt the oxidation process. This allows the tea to remain chemically very similar to fresh leaves and produces the lighter, complex flavor of tea.

4. The Science of Storage

Green tea is one of the least oxidized types of tea and is therefore quite susceptible to damage from improper storage. Theanine, catechins and Vitamin C are all present in high levels in green tea and are all vulnerable to oxidation. Storing green tea in an airtight container is recommended but hardly practical. The best strategy is to buy green tea in small, opaque, airtight packaging and use it within a few months. Do place open packages in a closed, opaque container and store in a cool, dark place free from moisture and strong odors.

5. A Formula for Success: H_2O pH = 7.9 - 8.2

The potential of hydrogen (pH) of water has a strong effect on the flavor of green tea. If the water is too acidic (below pH 7), the tea will taste sour. Natural spring water generally falls into the proper pH range for excellent tea. Be careful, however, to avoid spring waters with a high mineral content. Minerals like lime, calcium and magnesium can negatively affect the flavor of green tea. Charcoal activated filters can remove these, and other, impurities from your tap water without removing all the minerals. Completely mineral free water, like distilled water, should be avoided as it doesn't bring out the more subtle flavors of green tea. Try Eternal spring water for a perfectly pH balanced cup of tea.

6. The Bitter Beginning or the Bitter End

The most bitter components of green tea are caffeine ($C_8H_{10}N_4O_2$) and catechins. Very hot water, greater than 175 degrees Fahrenheit (80 C), radically extracts both compounds from green tea. If you pour boiling water over even the best green tea, the result will likely be a bitter brew. Over steeping green tea will also make it bitter as the woody tissues in the tea leaves will start to break down and release bitter flavors.

For less bitter result, make sure not to overheat your water—allow it to cool a little bit after boiling in order to avoid a pungently bitter taste.

7. Bitterness does not Mean Bad

In Japanese, there is a proverb saying "Good medicine taste bitter".
(良薬口に苦し)

Theanine is found in tea leaves that have grown under the shade and in young tea sprouts before harvest. According to Berkeley Wellness, this amino acid "appears to alter levels of various neurotransmitters, producing a calming effect" and according to WebMD, "people use Theanine for treating anxiety and blood pressure, for preventing Alzheimer's disease, and for making cancer drugs more effective." Because it relaxes the brain, nerves, and body, it serves well as a moderator to the effects of caffeine. This is why drinking tea with the same caffeine content as coffee has a steady and invigorating effect instead of a jittery one. In order to maximize the amount of Theanine in your Green Tea, it is recommended to brew the leaves in a lower temperature for a longer amount of time.

8. The Perfect Cup for the Perfect Cup

Serving green tea in a porcelain teacup is more than just aesthetically pleasing. The nonporous surface of the cup won't absorb polyphenols, allowing them to do their magic. Polyphenols, or natural plant compounds, stabilize plant colors and flavors and often have anti-oxidant properties. Porcelain teacups also have thin lips which deliver the tea to your tongue in the perfect manner. Coffee mugs are generally made of stoneware which is thicker and more porous than porcelain.

9. Does Hot Hit the Spot?

The temperature of green tea affects how its taste is perceived. A 2005 study found that taste receptor TRPM5 sends a stronger signal to the brain when foods are warmer. This receptor is responsible for the perception of sweet, bitter and umami flavors. If brewed correctly, green tea then will taste its best just after it is done seeping and before it gets too cool. If you want to be exact about it, most grocery retailers, like Target and Safeway, sell reasonably priced kitchen thermometers.

10. How Do You Take Your Tea?

Green tea purists would argue there is no need to add anything to a well-made cup. Chemists would ask you to weigh the evidence. While honey and other sweeteners don't seem to change the chemical make-up of green tea, lemon and milk do. Lemon juice stops polyphenols, like catechins, from binding with iron and calcium, thus making them more available for the body to use. Milk, on the other hand, seems to have the opposite effect and might reduce the bioavailability of polyphenols. Drop by your local farmer's market for some fresh honey and lemons but, for the best health benefit, skip the milk.

11. Balancing Flavor and Benefits

Catechins are known for their healthful benefits and their bitterness. You don't have to sacrifice flavor for health, however, as better quality green teas contain large amounts of amino acids and catechins. The savory flavor of the amino acids subdues the bitterness of the catechins. A 1975 study found that teas high in both catechins and amino acids scored high in tests with common people. The Tea Guardian compiled a nice list of high catechin green teas that are also flavorful.

12. Enjoy the Second Infusion

In Japan, it is common practice to do 2nd infusion to get 2nd cup. You can use the same green tea after pouring the first cup, and infuse one more time. The first infusion is called "Issenme", the second infusion is called "Nissenme". In order to get tastier 2nd infusion follow below steps.

SECTION 2

INTERMEDIATE VARIETY OF GREEN TEA DRINKS

05 How to Make Tasty Green Tea Latte

There are different ways to make a green tea latte, but all of them involve matcha, which is the fine powder made from grinding a special variety of green tea. It has two unique characteristics in its farming and processing: The first is that it's shade-grown for three weeks before it is harvested, and then when processed the stems and veins of the plant are removed. In other words, matcha is not simply ground green tea leaves of any variety. So if you want to make a delicious green tea latte, you will need real matcha.

How To Make A Traditional Hot Green Tea Latte

This method takes the most time, but will generally yield the best flavor. Start with a wide mug that's at least eight ounces in size. Using a fine sifter, sift about one teaspoon of matcha into the mug. The sifter helps break up clumps that may happen in storage. It's important to use wide mugs as the tools to make the latte work better with more room.

The next step is to heat some water. You can use either a tea kettle or a saucepan for this step, but the important thing is not to use boiling water in your latte. Remove 1/4 cup of water before it reaches a boil, or let the water stand after boiling for about a minute to reach the correct temperature. Boiling water will negatively affect the taste of the matcha and may make it taste harsh.

Pour the hot water into the mug with the matcha and then combine it into a paste. You can use either a whisk or a handheld frother for this step. Bamboo whisks are traditional and work the best, but the other methods will work as well. Make sure the end result is a smooth paste with no lumps.

At this point, you can heat up 3/4 cup of milk and one teaspoon of sweetener such as sugar or honey. Use more or less sweetener as desired. Any type of milk can be used, including non-dairy and low-fat milks. However, take note that low-fat milks will produce less foam and have a less rich taste. Full-fat cow's milk, coconut, or almond milk tend to work the best.

As with the water, do not let the milk boil. The best way to do this is to use a thermometer and only let it reach about 150 degrees Fahrenheit. In order to produce foam, you have a couple of options. If you have a handheld frother, you can run it for 30 seconds just below the surface of the warm milk. If you don't have a frother, you can whisk the milk after you pour it into your mug.

Speed It Up - A Hot Green Tea Latte Fast

If you have less time, you might want to consider the following faster method of making a green tea latte. In this method, you'll combine the 3/4 cup of milk with the 1/4 cup of water in a microwave-safe jar. Place it in the microwave uncovered and cook it for two minutes. Watch it carefully to make sure it doesn't boil.

When the milk and water mixture is hot, sift in one teaspoon of matcha and your desired amount of sweetener. In the quick method, it's better to use powdered sweetener such as sugar or a sugar alternative.

Seal and cover the jar, then shake it for a full minute. Make sure to use a towel or potholder to protect your hands. You can also use an immersion blender if the jar doesn't have a lid. You'll only need about 20 seconds on this method. This method doesn't look as pretty as the long way, but it should have a similar taste.

Cool It Down - Making An Iced Green Tea Latte

In the summer, an iced green tea latte is just the thing to cool down and still get the same calming energy of matcha. In this method, you'll need a cocktail shaker, a jar with a lid or a wide glass. Cocktail shakers work the best for creating froth and making your latte nice and cold.

Put one cup of ice into the cocktail shaker and then sift two teaspoons of matcha into the shaker. Add half a cup of water and half a cup of milk along with desired sweetener. Again, higher fat milks will produce more froth. Close the cocktail shaker and shake it for a full minute.

If you don't have a cocktail shaker, you

can combine the above ingredients except for the ice and either whisk or use
an immersion blender to mix.

Once the mixture is combined, you
can use it to create two smaller lattes
or one large one. Add ice to serving
glasses and strain the mixture from
the cocktail shaker into the glass. If you
used one of the other methods, then
simply pour it in. If the mixture isn't cold
enough, try chilling it for a few minutes
in the freezer first.

Iced green tea lattes are perfect with a
small amount of whip cream to finish.

Coffee House Green Tea Latte

Making a green tea latte similar to
those found at coffee houses such as
Starbucks differs only slightly from the
above methods. One difference is that
vanilla syrup is often used as a sweetener. In the case of an iced green tea
latte, you add about four teaspoons
of matcha powder to one cup of milk
and blend with a frother or electric
whisk. Then add one cup of ice and
mix in your desired amount of vanilla syrup. Starbucks uses a premade
blend of matcha powder and sugar
that goes into the cup first and is followed by steamed milk. Some coffee
houses also use premade matcha and
milk bases that can be added to ice,
blended with ice or heated up.

06 20 Yummy and Healthy Green Tea Smoothie Recipes – and Everything You Need to Know About Green Tea Smoothie

Green tea is one of the healthiest forms of hot tea. Not only does it help with general health, but it also tastes delicious. Green tea also comes in a variety of forms such as tea bags, loose leaves, and matcha. Each form has a slightly different taste, giving options for those who enjoy the taste of green tea and the health benefits it provides.

Green tea smoothies are also exceptionally delicious and are perfect for those who enjoy a little sweetness with their tea. The best part about making these delicious treats is, you can get creative with the process to make it your own creation.

Basic of Green Tea Smoothies

There are mainly two ways to make green tea smoothie:

o Approach 1 - Matcha Green Tea Smoothies

o Approach 2 - Loose Leaf Green Tea Smoothies

In this article, I will show you tips and trick of each approach along with recipes for each. Read on, or bookmark this page as this is the ultimate guide for making green tea smoothies.

Approach 1 - Matcha Green Tea Smoothies: The Quickest Green Tea Smoothie There is!

Matcha is a ground and powdered form of regular green tea leaves that are grown in the shade away from direct sunlight. It more resembles a protein powder or coffee grounds than green tea leaves, but the matcha retains all the healthy vitamins and minerals from the tea leaves. Making smoothies using matcha is a simple process, and with just a few ingredients, you can have a delicious smoothie packed with nutrients.green tea smoothies.

Matcha Making - Simply Explained

1. Tea is covered before harvesting

2. Tea is steamed and dried using special equipments

3. Veins and stems of leaf are separated by hand

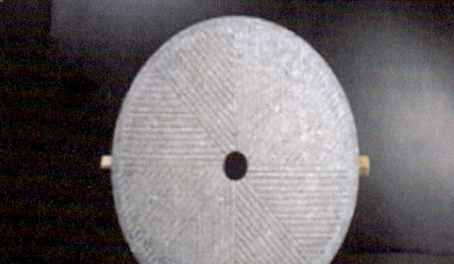

4. Stone mill used to grind the tea

5. Stone Grinding process makes tea into 4 micrometer

6. Resulting Matcha

Matcha is a ground, powdered form of Japanese Green Tea. A specific type of tea called Tencha is grown shaded prior to harvesting.

Making matcha green tea smoothies is simple. In fact, it is so simple, that it only takes a few minutes of your time each day to make the delicious treat. You simply need to scoop the ingredients you desire, and mix in the appropriate amount of matcha. Then, you will have the perfect green tea smoothie for your taste and preference.

There are several pros to the use of matcha in your green tea smoothie. For one, it is much faster than steeping your tea leaves or grinding them into a powder; the process is already finished for you. This makes getting your smoothie that much faster! Another pro of using matcha is the simplicity of the powder. For novice green tea drinkers, matcha might be the perfect choice to make their smoothies. It is a simple scoop instead of learning to grind your own. A disadvantage to using matcha in one's smoothies is the price. Matcha can be pricey in certain places. For some, it is much more cost effective to steep their own green tea leaves or grind them at home because they are grown in the shade throughout the entirety of the plant's life, it takes much longer to grow the green tea leaves which matcha is made from. This longer time span is what gives matcha is delicious and different flavor, but it is also the reason matcha can be quite pricey.

Approach 2 - Loose Leaf Green Tea Makes an Amazing and Delicious Smoothie!

There are two ways to use loose green tea leaves to make a smoothie. Both ways create a different taste and texture, and neither is difficult to learn. Either way is just as effective as the other, but, depending on your preference, you can choose which is better or easier for you. The two ways to prepare your green tea for the smoothie are as follows:

Steep your green tea leaves just as you would if you were to drink it straight. Allow it to cool slightly, then, pour it into the blender on top of your other ingredients.

Grind your green tea leaves until they are finely powdered—or powdered to your preference. A coffee grinder is a good and easy option to grind green tea. Grinding regular loose leaf green tea does not make matcha since matcha is made of specific tea type called "Tencha" which is different from loose leaf green tea you usually get from store. Ground tea leaves are called "Konacha" in Japan. Then, place the ground tea leaves into the blender to be made into a smoothie.

Still tasty, but not as bitter as Matcha and it also tastes different.

If you want to make your own matcha, Sharp TE-T56U-GR Tea-Cere Matcha Tea Maker allows you to grind green tea the way you traditionally would using stone mill. This machine uses ceramic to mimic the traditional stone mill. Note that you need to use specific type of green tea called "Tencha" in order to get resulting Matcha. Either process makes delicious smoothies, so once your tea is prepared, you can add the same ingredients as your matcha smoothie, or get creative and experiment. A pro of this using tea leaves is more cost effective than using store-bought matcha. The loose tea isn't as costly as matcha, and it is easier to find in stores across the United States. On the other hand, using loose te leaves requires more time than using store-bought matcha, as it takes longer to steep the tea or grind the leaves. It takes longer to steep the tea or grind the leaves than it does to simply scoop matcha.

TE-T56U- GR Tea-Cere Matcha Tea Maker

There Are too Many Options. Which One is Right for Me?

How do you choose which method is right for you? If you are new to green tea, it might be easier to purchase matchato make your smoothies. The health benefits are the same, but the process is a bit simpler than using loose leaves. If you are concerned about cost, it might be a better choice to go with the loose leaves. But, what if you are unable to grind the loose leaves? Then you might consider steeping the leaves or purchasing matcha for your smoothies. If time is a concern, then you might choose to use matcha for your tea. If you already have loose leaves in your kitchen, then you might consider either steeping or grinding. Your taste

1. Quick Green Smoothie

When green tea is combined with spinach, the health benefits are both tremendous and varied. Spinach contains vitamins and iron. The addition of banana brings some much-needed potassium to this recipe and the grapes give the smoothie some delicious sweetness.

o 2 cups of frozen green grapes
o 1 frozen banana
o 1 cup of baby spinach leaves
o 2 Tablespoon of Matcha Green Tea Powder

Combine all the ingredients in a blender and blend until smooth.

2. Refreshing Peach Green Tea Smoothie

Peaches provide the body with fiber, antioxidants, and a whopping ten vitamins. The banana will give the body a healthy dose of potassium.

o 1 frozen banana
o 1 large peach, pitted, skinned, and cut into large chunks
o 2 tbsp. of Matcha Green Tea Powder
o 1 tbsp. of maple syrup

53

3. Banana and Peanut Butter Green Tea Smoothie

Bananas offer high levels of potassium, an essential electrolyte. Peanut butter gives the body a boost of protein.

o 1 frozen banana
o 1/2 cup of milk
o 2 tbsp. of peanut butter
o 1 tbsp. of maple syrup
o 2 tbsp. of Matcha Green Tea Powder

Combine all the ingredients in a blender and blend until smooth.
.

4. Apple, Lemon, and Ginger Green Tea Smoothie

Ginger acts as an anti-inflammatory to the digestive system while lemon's antibacterial properties clean out the body.

o 1 frozen apple

o 1 2-inch chunk of ginger, peeled and loosely chopped
o 2 tbsp. of lemon juice
o 1 tbsp. of honey
o 2 Tablespoon of Matcha Green Tea Powder

5. Blueberry and Flaxseed Green Tea Smoothie

Blueberries provide the body with high levels of Vitamin C. Flaxseeds are full of fiber to aid your digestive system.

o 1 tbsp. of flaxseeds
o 1 cup of frozen blueberries

o 1/2 cup of Greek yogurt
o 1 tbsp, of honey
o 2 Tablespoon of Matcha Green Tea Powder

Combine all the ingredients in a blender and blend until smooth.

6. Tropical Pineapple Green Tea Smoothie

Pineapples are full of essential electrolytes that will keep your body feeling great all day long.

o 1 cup of pineapple chunks
o 2 tbsp. of lemon juice
o 1/2 cup of coconut milk

o 1 tbsp. of honey
o 1 cup of ice
o 2 tbsp. of Matcha Green Tea Powder

Combine all the ingredients in a blender and blend until smooth.

7. Green Goddess Green Tea Smoothie

Avocados give the body essential fatty acids while bananas provide the body with a daily serving of potassium.

o 1 avocado, peeled, pitted and cut into quarters
o 2 tbsp. of lemon juice
o 1 frozen banana
o 1 tbsp. of honey
o 1/2 cup of ice
o 2 tbsp. of Matcha Green Tea Powder

Combine all the ingredients in a blender and blend until smooth.

8. Super Green Smoothie

The high amount of greens in this recipe will give your body loads of iron and vitamin A.

o 1 cup of baby spinach leaves
o 1/2 cup of baby kale leaves
o 6 large fresh mint leaves

o 1 frozen banana
o 1 tbsp. of maple syrup
o 2 tbsp. of Matcha Green Tea Powder

Combine all the ingredients in a blender and blend until smooth.

9. Orange and Mango Green Tea Smoothie

Oranges offer the body high levels of Vitamin C while bananas provide potassium.

o 3/4 cup of freshly squeezed orange juice
o 1 cup of frozen mango chunks
o 1 frozen banana
o 2 tbsp. of Matcha Green Tea Powder

Combine all the ingredients in a blender and blend until smooth.

10. Berry & Green Tea Smoothie

Berries are packed with antioxidants and offer delicious sweetness to this recipe.

o 1 cup of frozen assorted berries
o 1 tsp of lemon juice
o 1 frozen banana
o 1/2 cup of Greek yogurt
o 1/2 cup of brewed green tea that has been refrigerated for one hour

Combine all the ingredients in a blender and blend until smooth.

61

11. Apple Pie Green Tea Smoothie

This dessert-like smoothie is full of protein and fiber.

o 1/2 cup of rolled oats
o 1 apple, peeled, pitted and cut into chunks
o 1 tsp of vanilla extract

o 1/2 cup of Greek yogurt
o 1/2 cup of ice
o 1/2 cup of brewed green tea that has been refrigerated for one hour
Combine all the ingredients in a blender and blend until smooth..

12. Strawberry Banana Green Tea Smoothie

Packed with antioxidants and potassium, this smoothie is a sweet treat.

o 1 cup of frozen strawberries
o 1 frozen banana
o 1/2 cup of Greek yogurt

o 1/2 cup of ice
o 1/3 cup of brewed green tea that has been refrigerated for one hour

Combine all the ingredients in a blender and blend until smooth.

13. Carrot and Ginger Green Tea Smoothie

Carrots are full of nutrients like beta-carotene and fiber. Ginger aids the digestive system.

o 1 peeled and chopped carrot
o 1 pear, peeled, pitted and roughly chopped
o 1 2-inch chunk of ginger, peeled and chopped
o 1/2 cup of ice
o 1/3 cup of brewed green tea that has been refrigerated for one hour

Combine all the ingredients in a blender and blend until smooth.

14. Apple and Chia Seed Green Tea Smoothie

Chia seeds are full of protein and fiber. Apples provide vitamin C as well as extra sweetness.

o 2 tbsp. of chia seeds
o 1 apple, peeled, pitted and roughly chopped
o 1 tsbp. of lemon juice
o 1 cup of ice
o 1/2 cup of plain yogurt
o 1/2 cup of brewed green tea that has been refrigerated for one hour
Combine all the ingredients in a blender and blend until smooth.

15. Papaya and Strawberry Green Tea Smoothie

Strawberries give the body antioxidants while papaya provides enzymes that aid in digestion.

o 1 cup of frozen papaya chunks
o 1 cup of frozen strawberries
o 1 ripe banana
o 1 tbsp. of honey
o 1/2 cup of brewed green tea that has been refrigerated for one hour

Combine all the ingredients in a blender and blend until smooth

16. Pear and Almond Green Tea Smoothie

Almonds provide lots of protein to the body and are full of vitamins. This smoothie will leave you feeling satisfied for hours.

o 1/2 cup of almonds
o 1 frozen pear, peeled and pitted
o 1 frozen banana
o 1/2 cup of brewed green tea that has been refrigerated for one hour
Combine all the ingredients in a high-powered blender like a vitamix and blend until smooth.

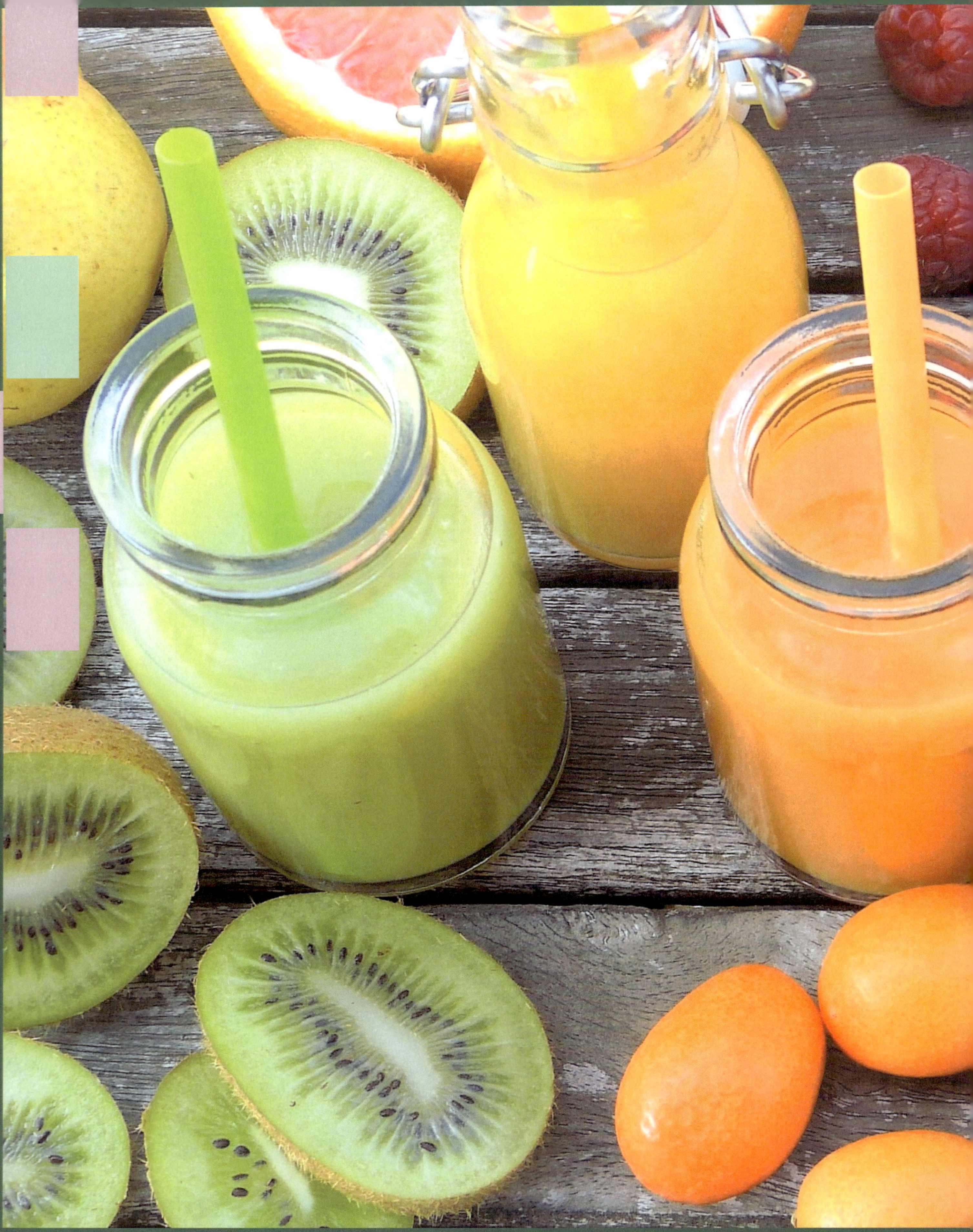

17. Island Green Tea Smoothie

These tropical ingredients give the body fiber and vitamin C.

o 1/2 cup of frozen mango chunks
o 3/4 cup of pineapple chunks
o 1 frozen banana

o 1 tosp. of honey
o 1/3 cup of coconut milk
o 1/2 cup of brewed green tea that has been refrigerated for one hour

Combine all the ingredients in a blender and blend until smooth.

18. Raspberry, Lime and Mint Green Tea Smoothie

This refreshing smoothie offers anti-oxidants and vitamin C.

o 1 cup of frozen raspberries
o 3 tbsp. of lime juice
o 3 tbsp. of chopped fresh mint leaves
o 1 tbsp. of honey
o 1/2 cup of orange juice
o 1/2 cup of ice
o 1/3 cup of brewed green tea that has been refrigerated for one hour

Combine all the ingredients in a blender and blend until smooth.

19. Chocolate Banana Green Tea Smoothie

Decadent chocolate gives the body a boost of magnesium.

o 1/4 cup of cocoa powder
o 1 1/2 frozen bananas
o 2 tbsp of almond butter
o 1 tbsp of honey
o 1/2 cup of milk
o 1/2 cup of ice
o 1/3 cup of brewed green tea that has been refrigerated for one hour

Combine all of the ingredients in a blender and blend until smooth.

Tip for Making Tastier Green Tea Smoothie

Use Covered Green Tea

For loose leaf green tea smoothies, liked to use covered Japanese green tea which has the best health benefits and a bright emerald green color. Covered green tea has a brighter color which makes the smoothie look better. Click here to get covered Japanese Green Tea.

Use a Good Mixer for Ice Crushing

If you are using blender which can crush ice such as a Vitamix, add a cup of crushed ice in addition to the ingredients for better taste. Please note that regular mixer usually does not crush ice, so you have to get a mixer which can crush ice. I use a Vitamix which is the company that makes mixers for Frappuccino® at Starbucks and Jumba Juice. Vitamix is a bit pricier than other mixers, but it's very durable and lasts long. Click here to get Vitamix from Amazon.

73

Use Culinary Grade Matcha

There are different types of matcha available in the market. The two main types you find are Culinary Grade Matcha (AKA Cooking Mathca) and Ceremonial Grade Matcha. Culinary Grade is most often used for cooking such that the matcha is mixed with other recipes to make smoothie, cookies, cakes etc.; this is the type used by most retailers such as Starbucks when they say matcha in their product name. Ceremonial Grade Matcha is usually more expensive and uses younger tea leaves, and the stems and veins are removed in the process of making them. Ceremonial Grade is used in tea ceremonies and many tea masters suggest only to mix it with hot water for "ceremonial" purposes. I personally think that both taste good, but Culinary Grade Matcha usually have stronger flavor which comes out better in smoothie and is more economical.

74

Looking for More Ways to Enjoy Green Tea Smoothies? Here are Links to Other Great Green Tea Smoothie Recipes

There are many great Green Tea Smoothie recipes out there, and here is a list of my favorites.

o Green Tea Smoothie with Banana with Video by Just One Cookbook This is my favorite blog, she creates amazing video for many of Japanese Recipes. This one also has a video of how to make green tea smoothie with banana.

o Exotic Green Smoothie, Dairy-Free Coconut Matcha Smoothie by Jen Yee This is a recipe from Food Republic I personally like. The recipe is from Jen Yee, Award Winning Chef at NYC's Lafayette Grand Cafe and Bakery.

o Peach Green Tea Smoothie and Green Tea and Almond Smoothie by Janette's Healthy Living

My another favorite recipe blog features two green tea smoothie recipe.

o Mango Green Tea Smoothie by Cooking Classy Another lovely recipe blog with beautiful images.

o Matcha Mango Pineapple Smoothie by Teacups & Things

Her blog and recipes are beautifully done with nice images. I love her simple style of the clean blogo

o Mint and Green Tea Smoothie by

Kitchen Konfidence

Brandon is a photographer and cook, his recipes are very personal and his photography passion shows on each recipe.

o Raspberry Green Tea Smoothie by Recipe Runner

Image of this recipe is so cute! Dinae's love of cooking and running show a very unique perspective on how she writes about her recipe.

o 30 Fat Burning Detox Green Tea Smoothie Recipe

They have 30 different links specific to detoxing with green tea smoothie.

07 Do The Dos And Don'ts Of Green Tea Smoothies

Green Tea is a truly remarkable beverage. It isn't only versatile and delicious, it's also extremely beneficial for your health and wellness. Green tea's bioactive compounds are a goldmine of antioxidants and other nutrients that are known to foster fat loss, improve brain function and even lower the risk of cancer, among many other perks, such as killing bacteria and improving dental health.

You can enjoy the benefits of green tea by drinking a few cups per day, but this is not the only way to enjoy the taste and the beneficial properties that come with it. Why not infusing a smoothie with the aroma, and unmistakable taste of green tea?

This article will get you through a few tips, dos, don'ts and other secrets to make the perfect green tea.

Add Cooled Green Tea Gradually

Make sure you never use hot tea to make a smoothie: hot liquids might disrupt certain ingredients in your smoothie and turn everything in a watery blend. The best thing to do is to brew your desired amount of green tea the night earlier and let it chill overnight. By letting the tea sit for a few hours, you will allow the flavors to settle in more intensely. To achieve the best balance and the most suitable consistency for your smoothie, it is a great idea to add the tea gradually. If you take it one step at a time, you will also be able to add more, if you want to increase the green tea punch of the smoothie, or if you simply want to make it less thick. By adding all the tea at once, you risk going a bit overboard with the balance, and you might also ruin the texture and consistency of your smoothie! Make sure to always add a bit in, keep mixing, and add more if needed!

Green Tea Goes Great With Fruit

Green tea has a very distinctive flavor profile, and for better or for worse, it will end up being the defining "note" of your smoothie. Since green tea has such a strong, prominent and characteristic flavor, it is important to pair it with suitable ingredients. The possibilities are truly endless. Fruit is always a good choice, and it could help you make some interesting combinations. If you are looking for something summery and exotic, try watermelon. If you are keen on something zesty and bold, lemon or lime will certainly hit the spot. On the other hand, you can achieve tantalizing results with fruits that are well-known for their sweetness and balance, including blueberries, bananas, peaches and even apricots.

Make Your Green Tea Smoothies A Nutrient Powerhouse

If you are looking for a smoothie that packs a huge wellness punch, try blending in some of your favorite greens! You can make a delicious health-conscious smoothie by blending green tea with spinach, which is a great source of iron and antioxidants. Or you can pair it with avocados, which feature healthy dietary fibers, non-saturated fatty acids and tons of amazing nutrients. For a hint of sweetness, grapes or honey can help!

Try Roots, For A Surprising Smoothie

lGreen tea mixes really well with roots, spices and other herbs. Mint and even fresh basil might do wonders. You can also try some ginger, which is also well-known for its beneficial health effects.

A Little Sugar Never Hurt Nobody

If you are looking for a creamy, rewarding and rich consistency, try adding some yogurt, or even some ice cream, if you are feeling particularly indulgent. Some plain milk or vanilla-flavored ice cream, are great choices. As mentioned earlier, green tea generally has a very strong, distinctive and somewhat imposing flavor: you want to have a smoothie where it is the absolute star at the forefront of the picture, so it is important to pick other ingredients that embrace its qualities. If you are feeling particularly decadent, and if you think you really deserve a treat, try the following smoothie idea: blend in some green tea with some vanilla ice cream, a bit of yogurt, a hint of lime and some dates. Serve, and sprinkle the top with graham cookie crumbles and chocolate drops! Some wouldn't really call it a smoothie, but hey, who are we to judge? The beauty of smoothies is that you can completely tailor them to the occasion. They can be as healthy and essential as you want them to be, or they can be lavish, indulgent and decadent.

Pour In A Little Matcha Powder

Some people like to use matcha green tea powder instead of brewing tea in order to make a smoothie. Adding the powder can help you save more time and add that green tea flavor to your smoothie, even when you don't have time to brew tea and let it chill over the course of several hours. Matcha is a different compared to your average green tea. Let us explain. Unlike the tea you find offered as a loose-leaf option, Matcha is a powder made of tea leaves which have been grown in the shades and sheltered from direct sunlight throughout the entire lifespan of the plant. As a result of this, tea plants grow much slower, which means that they produce higher chlorophyll levels in their leaves. This is the reason why matcha leaves usually appear more intensely green! Nonetheless, matcha does make an interesting twist on your green tea smoothie, and it is worth a try.

These are only a few of the many amazing possibilities: what's your favorite green smoothie recipe?

08 20 Trendy Green Tea Cocktail Recipes

Green tea and matcha aren't just for ceramic tea mugs anymore. Bartenders across the nation have been using green tea and matcha in their trendy recipes, and it's been a great success.

Here are 20 trendy and tasty cocktail recipes for any bartender to wow their friends and guests – all these recipes use matcha powder and prepared green tea

1. Mango With a Green Tea Splash

Fill a shaker with ice and 1 1/2 parts apple juice, 1 1/2 parts Bison Grass Flavored Vodka, 1/3 parts green mint liqueur, 1/3 green banana syrup, and 1/3 parts Pisang Ambon. Shake and strain into a cool cocktail glass.

2. Vodka and Green Tea Cooler

Fill a highball glass with ice cubes. Add 1 1/2 parts vodka, 1 1/2 parts green tea, 1/2 part pomegranate juice, 1/2 part simple syrup, and 1 twist lemon. Stir. Garnish with a lemon wedge. Add flavored vodka such as Smirnoff pomegranate or passion fruit for a more unique flavor.

3. Green Tea Martini

Fill a shaker with ice and 1 1/2 parts apple juice, 1 1/2 parts Bison Grass Flavored Vodka, 1/3 parts green mint liqueur, 1/3 green banana syrup, and 1/3 parts Pisang Ambon. Shake and strain into a cool cocktail glass.

4. Almond Green Iced Tea

Fill a highball glass with ice cubes. Add 4
parts green tea, 1/2 lemon juice, and 1/2
part Orgeat Almond Syrup. Stir and garnish
with a lemon wedge.

5. Matcha Highball

Combine 2 ounces of Japanese whiskey, 1/2 ounce of lemon juice, 1/2 ounce of honey syrup, and 1/4 teaspoon of matcha green tea powder in a cocktail shaker. Shake thoroughly, and pour into a cool and ice-filled collins glass Pour 4 ounces of cold club soda into the shaker and swirl to loosen the leftover matcha powder. Pour into the glass and stir. Garnish with a lemon wheel.

6. Matcha and Gin

Add 1/2 teaspoon of matcha powder, 1 ounce of lemon juice, 2 ounces of gin, 4 teaspoons of simple syrup, and a dash of bitters. Add ice and shake. Strain into a cold glass.

7. Matcha Gimlet

In a glass, mix 1/2 ounce of matcha powder with 1/3 a cup of water until well blended. Add 1 ounce of lime juice and 1/2 an ounce of simple syrup. Pour into a shaker with 2 1/2 ounces of gin and ice. Shake until cold. Strain into a cold martini glass.

8. Green Tea and Cucumber Martini

Muddle a 2 inch piece of cucumber and a piece of fresh ginger with a dash of salt and a dash of simple syrup. Add 2 ounces of citrus flavored vodka (Belvedere or Smirnoff), 3/4 ounce of green tea, and two basil leaves. Strain into a cold martini glass and garnish with a cucumber slice.

91

9. Green Tea Vodka Spritzer

Add 2 ice cubes, 2 limes worth of lime juice, 1 ounce vodka, 2 ounces of green tea, and a splash of Canada Dry ginger ale. Stir and garnish with a slice of lime.

10. Green Tea Apple Cocktail

Rim a cocktail glass with sugar and fill with ice. Pour 1 ounce of vodka, 1/2 cup of apple cider, and fill the remainder of the glass with green tea. Garnish with an apple slice.

11. Green Tea Cosmo

In an ice filled shaker, add 2 ounces green tea, 1 ounce vodka, 1/2 ounce orange liqueur, 1/2 ounce lime juice, and 1/2 ounce of cranberry juice cocktail. Shake and then strain into a cold martini glass. Garnish with a lime peel.

12. Habanero Green Tea Shooters- Makes 10 shots

Combine 1/2 cup vodka and 1/2 teaspoon chili habanero pepper in a small bowl. Let sit for 20 minutes. Strain out the pepper. Pour tablespoon of vodka mixture into 10 cold shotglasses and add one watermelon or honeydew melon ball to each glass. Pour 1 tablespoon of Lipton Sparkling Green Tea (use berry or strawberry kiwi for a variety)into each. Garnish with cilantro sprig and serve.

13. Green Tea and Pumpkin Cocktail

Rim old fashioned glass with a sugar cinnamon mixture. Fill a shaker with ice and add 1 cup of green tea, 1 tablespoon pumpkin puree, 1/4 teaspoon of sugar, and 1 1/2 ounces of vodka. Shake and strain over ice.

14. Green Tea Whiskey

Fill a highball glass with ice. Add 1 1/2 ounces of whiskey and fill with green tea. Garnish with a lime wedge

15. Green Tea Mojito

Muddle 4 mint leaves with 2 teaspoons of sugar in a highball glass. Add ice and stir in the 1/2 cup of green tea and 1 tablespoon of lime juice.

16. Honey Bee Green Tea

Fill a highball glass with ice. Add 1 ounce honey liqueur. Then, fill the glass with brewed green tea and garnish with a lemon wedge.

17. Cognac Ginger Green Tea

In a mixing glass, add 3 pieces of ginger, 3 mint leaves, and 1/2 ounce of simple syrup and muddle. Pour 1 ounce of Cognac and 2 ounces of green tea and muddle a little more. Strain into an ice-filled high ball glass. Garnish with a mint leaf.

18. Bourbon Green Tea

In a double old fashioned glass, add 1 1/2 ounces of bourbon whiskey and 1/2 ounce of limoncello. Fill with ice and top with 4 ounces of green tea. Garnish with a lemon wedge.

19. Matcha Lemon Drop

Rim a cocktail glass with sugar. Set aside. Microwave 1/2 cup of water and 1/2 cup of honey until combined (30 seconds). Combine 3/4 ounces of this honey water, 3/4 ounces of lemon juice, 1/4 teaspoon of matcha powder, and 2 ounces of vodka in a shaker. Fill with ice and shake until smooth. Strain into the glass and Garnish with lemon twist.

20. Matcha Banana Cream

Shake with ice 1 ounce of banana liqueur, 1 ounce creme de cacao, 1/2 teaspoon of matcha powder, 1 ounce of vodka, and 2 ounces of half and half. Strain into a cocktail glass and serve.

Try out each of these easy to make recipes and unique flavors that make use of a v64ariety of ingredients. Anyone is sure to find one recipe among these that they love!

09 Green Tea Bubble Tea What is it? Why Is It Trending? And How You Can Make It At Home (Guest Author from CEO of BubbleTeaOlogy Inc.)

When most people think of bubble tea they think of the boba or tapioca pearls on the bottom of the cup. But actually, bubble tea got its name because of the small bubbles that form on top after shaking the tea. In fact, In Taiwan (where bubble tea was invented) the most popular drink isn't boba milk tea but actually regular iced green or oolong tea. Green tea is often seen as a healthier option than coffee and can be very refreshing on hot summer days.

Green Tea Bubble Tea is simply shaken iced green tea. Most shops in Taiwan will start with hot green tea, add ice and then shake it in a shaker machine for about 6-8 seconds to create the bubbles on top.

Green Tea Bubble Milk Teas

While most milk tea is made by mixing fresh milk with black tea, many people are also mixing milk with green tea or matcha which can then be served either hot or cold. One of my favorites is a matcha bubble tea latte which combines matcha powder, fresh milk and tapioca pearls to make an unforgettable crink.

Bubble Milk Tea in the US is usually made by using a flavored powder. For example, to make taro bubble tea, most shops will use taro bubble tea powder. Surprisingly, some bubble tea shops mix this powder with water so there isn't actually any tea in your bubble tea! We recommend mixing taro powder with hot green tea to really accentuate the flavor.

HOW TO MAKE
GREEN TEA BUBBLE
MILK TEA AT HOME

To get started, you'll need a few things:

• Tapioca Pearls (You can be purchased on Amazon here. This is one I personally recommend)
https://www.amazon.com/gp/product/B003IHC294/ref=as_li_tl?ie=UTF8&camp=1789&creative=9325&creativeASIN=B003I-HC294&linkCode=as2&tag=green-tea08b-20&linkId=794475ba4ca-203f52086eac61fc435d8

• A large pot (with a lid)
• A serving bowl
• Honey
• High Quality Matcha (You can try our premium Matcha.)

Steps to make Green Tea Bubble Milke Tea

1. Measure 100 grams of tapioca pearls

2. Put 1000ml of water into a pot and bring it to a boil

3. Place the tapioca pearls into the water

4. Wait for the tapioca pearls to rise to the top and start to boil

5. Once the tapioca pearls begin to boil, stir them and start a timer for 25 minutes

6. Lower the heat to medium and stir occasionally

While your boba are boiling, start to prepare your honey

7. our 50 grams of honey into a bowl, add a little hot water and stir

8. Once the timer goes off, turn off the heat and let the tapioca pearls sit fcr 10 minutes with the lid on

9. After 10 minutes, put the tapioca pearls into a colander and rinse them with cold water until the tapioca balls are no longer hot

10. Let all the water drain from the strainer and put them in the bowl of honey

11. Let them soak for at least 20 minutes before serving

12. Place them in a cup and then add your favorite premium Matcha for homemade Green Tea Bubble Tea!

THE RISING TREND
OF BUBBLE TEA

Although bubble tea has been around since the 1980s it's still gaining in popularity.

People used to have to go to Los Angeles or New York for great bubble tea, now it's popping up in shopping malls all over the midwest and becoming as ubiquitous as Cinnabon or Jamba Juice.

As of November 2017, there are 1968 listings for bubble tea shops in the US and Google Trends reports continued growth in searches for bubble tea (the annual dips are during the winter months).

Bubble Tea is Trending in USA.

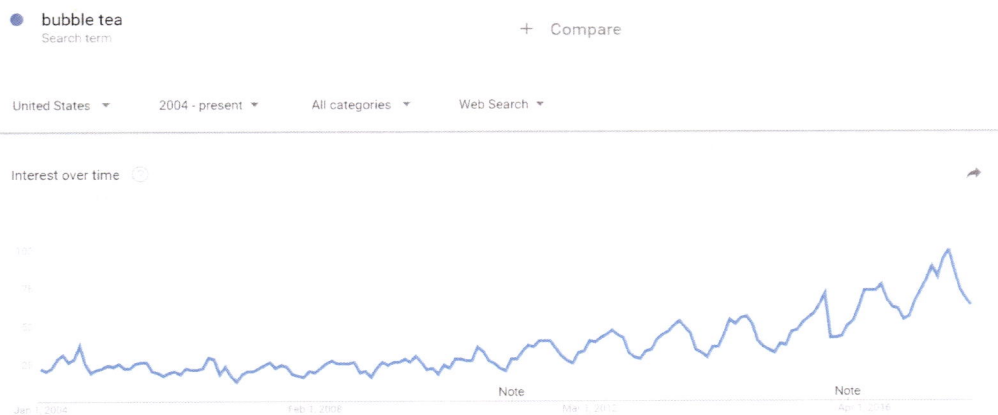

● **bubble tea**
  Search term

  ＋ Compare

United States ▾   2004 - present ▾   All categories ▾   Web Search ▾

Interest over time ⓘ

Jan 1, 2004   Feb 1, 2008   Mar 1, 2012   Apr 1, 2016
                              Note   Note

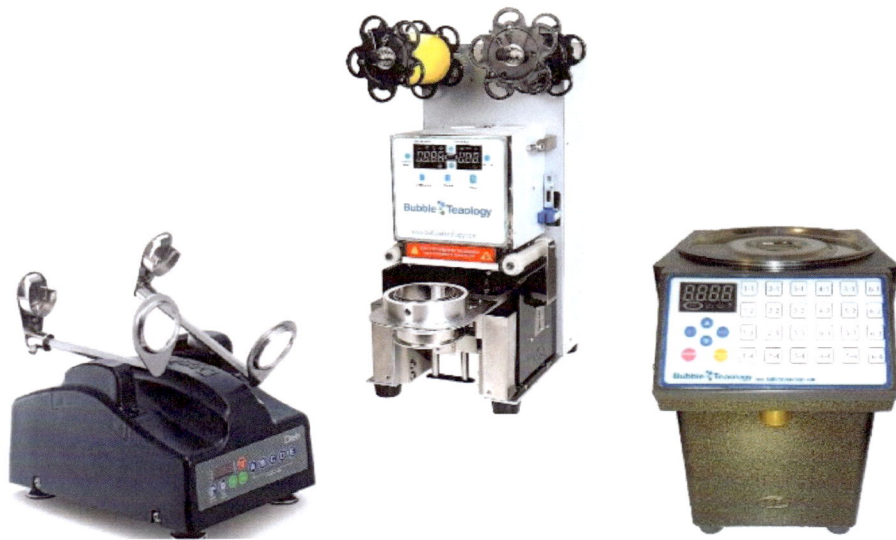

Going Pro

While making bubble tea at home can be a fun hobby, many people are capitalizing on the growing trend of bubble tea by opening their own bubble tea shop. Some of the professional equipment and machines that bubble tea shops are using are Cup Sealer Machines, Shaker Machines and Fructose Dispensers.

Japanese Green Tea readers can get a special discount of $75.00 on all bubble tea machines by using the code greentea ct BubbleTeaology.com.

This article is written by Mike, CEO of BubbleTeaology.

Mike is originally from the US but has spent the past 6 years in Taiwan and 2 of those years working for one of the largest bubble tea shops in Taiwan. Now he is the owner of BubbleTeaology which supplies Boba Tea Machines and Wholesale Ingredients to drink shops around the world.

Section 3

THE ADVANCED COOK WITH GREEN TEA

10 What You Should Know About Using Green Tea For Bread Baking

The best part about baking is the creative freedom of making something one of a kind with your own hands. Choosing your favorite fresh ingredients and trying new things leads to delicious discoveries about taste and health. Adding green tea or matcha to baked bread is a great way to incorporate a tasty superfood that you already know and love to your diet. Fresh tea leaves are not usually what comes to mind when choosing ingredients to bake bread, but many bakers across the world have already found the pleassure of baking

with tea. Although an uncommon bread ingredient for most, green tea can lend not only benefits of unique earthy flavor, but also incredible health benefits as well. The versatility of this superfood ingredient in bread baking alone is almost as impressive as the complete nutrition it provides the body and mind. A suggestion for balancing out the earthy, sometimes bitter flavor of green tea or matcha is by adding sweetening. Raw sugar, honey, agave and maple syrup all compliment the flavor and aroma that green tea presents and are easy to add to a bread recipe. This tip can be used in sweet or savory bread alike. Adding a pinch of extra salt along with a sweet component to a savory bread recipe will allow the flavors to bring out the best in one another, adding complexity and depth to a fresh, homemade baked bread. Whether you only have matcha on hand or simply prefer to use loose tea leaves, either can be incorporated into a freshly baked bread. Great matcha

often comes with a large price tag, and loose green tea leaf is more likely to be affordable. Be aware of the potency in both aroma and flavor of the amount of tea you choose to bake with, taking into account the matcha provides a more robust flavor in the finished bread. If you usually cook with fresh tea leaves, using the same amount when baking with matcha would not be wise! You will end up with a rich aroma but an overwhelming, unpleasant flavor! The best way to get the most delightful flavor is by using the freshest green tea or matcha available. Use according to your personal preference when baking for friends and family.

Ground matcha is subtle enough that it can be mixed in directly without causing issues with bread texture if done carefully and correctly. The most simplistic way to incorporate matcha into freshly baked bread is by mixing it in entirely with the dry ingredients. On the other hand, matcha can be known to slump significantly. Whisking the soft powder into a liquid is a little tip that will discourage heavy clumping that results in uneven flavor distribution throughout the bread. Whichever method you use, be sure that the matcha is wholly mixed in or dissolved. Although matcha is flavorful enough to not necessarily need to be steeped or infused, attempting this in your baking process cannot hurt and may even yield satisfying results so feel free to give it a try.

When it comes to baking, infusing green tea or matcha does not have to compromise the soft, chewy texture of fresh bread. The following methods are helpful in achieving perfect bread baked using green tea. Loose green tea leaf can be ground but may come coarse and noticeable in the finished bread. It should be noted that powdered green tea is interchangeable with fresh ground green tea in a bread recipe, but the powdered tea will be much smoother and possibly more concentrated than regular green tea, affecting the overall flavor and outcome of your bread. If coarsely ground leaves are the only option, add them to

the dough through brewing and straining through a cheesecloth to remove any possibility of grit. Steeping or infusing the fresh tea leaves is a better way of adding the benefits of tea into your baking.

This can be done with melted butter, hot milk or hot water, dependent upon the recipe. When infused with hot water, simply steep the tea as you usually would and add the mixture at the temperature that correlates with the recipe. Introducing hot milk should be done slowly and carefully since milk tends to boil over quickly. Once the milk begins to boil, control the temperature to a low simmer for five minutes. Set aside the milk and continue steeping until the desired aroma is present.

Start out with melted butter on a medium flame and add the tea to begin a tea infused butter for your baking recipe. After 10-15 minutes and occasional stirring, reduce the heat to low for another 10-15 minutes. Remove the mixture from heat and immediately strain out the tea before the butter begins to solidify. It is ready to bake

You've probably savored green tea brewed hot and loose leaf, into a warming beverage swimming with depth, ancient history, and culture. Or, perhaps you've even enjoyed it cold, iced, and with fresh lemon on an unsettling warm spring afternoon, or scooped up in the form of ice cream at your favorite sushi joint. But, have you ever had it in bread form? If not, you are missing out.

112

1. Matcha-Milk Tangzhong Bread

This type of bread uses Tangzhong roux (also called a water roux) to create a treat with a satisfying, pillowy give and pull-apart wonderfulness. Tangzhong roux is a flour and water roux added to yeast bread recipes in order to give it a lighter feel and further sustain its shelf life. Take note, because it's an important component in many of these breads-- but no fretting, it's way easier to make than you may think.

Yields one standard (8½" x 4½") loaf
To make the Tangzhong:
- 1/3 cup bread flour
- 1 cup water
To make the dough:
- 2 + ½ cups bread flour (you'll need bread flour for both the tangzhong and the dough)
- 1 large egg
- 2 tablespoons sugar (if you want a bread that is more of a dessert-oriented loaf, increase this to 4 tablespoons)
- ½ cup milk
- 2 teaspoons instant yeast
- 120 grams tangzhong (just a little over half of the above recipe)
- 3 tablespoons butter (softened at room temperature)
- 2 tablespoons matcha powder
- Egg wash (1 egg whisked with a tablespoon of milk or water)

Making the tangzhong:

1. In a heavy-bottomed saucepan, stir flour into water until it has completely dissolved and there are no lumps.

2. Set the pan on the stove at medium heat and begin to stir. Stir constantly until the mixture begins to thicken in order to prevent burning. Keep stirring until the mixture forms lines behind where your spoon has stirred. The desired consistency should be one that is somewhat thick, creamy, and smooth with no discernible grittiness.

3. Immediately transfer your tangzhong to a bowl to stop the cooking process and allow it to cool. Gently press cellophane onto the surface to prevent the

114

tangzhong from forming a skin, and allow it to cool to room temperature before using, or, place it in the fridge up for to 2 days if not using right away. The roux will only keep for several days after being made, so be sure to use it up quickly!

Making the dough:

1. In the bowl of a standing mixer (hand-held mixers might not be able to handle this job), combine the flour, sugar, and instant yeast. With your fist, form a well in the center, then add in your milk, egg, and tangzhong.

2. Use a spoon to incorporate the ingredients together until a shaggy (kind of wispy, kind of clumpy) dough is formed. Then, add in the butter and attach the bowl to the standing mixer.

3. Using a dough hook (an attachment made specifically for mixers to use as opposed to hand-kneading bread), knead the dough on medium speed for about 10 minutes, or until the dough is smooth. To check if the dough is ready, take a chunk and carefully stretch it thin until it breaks. When it breaks, a circular hole-like shape should appear on the stretched dough.

4. Remove the dough from the bowl and gently knead it into a circle by hand. Split the ball of dough in half, returning one half into the mixing bowl while reattaching it to the standing mixer; the other half goes into a lightly greased large bowl to proof.

5. Add matcha powder to the mixing bowl and continue kneading with the dough hook for about 2 minutes at medium speed, or until the matcha powder is thoroughly incorporated. The result should be a gorgeous springtime green. Transfer this dough into another lightly greased bowl, cover with cellophane, and leave to proof alongside the plain dough for about 60 minutes, until it has doubled in size.

6. Once both dough rounds have reached their first rise, transfer to a clean surface. Knead the dough rounds briefly, and divide each into four equal portions. Knead each portion into balls, cover with cellophane, and allow them to rest for 15 minutes to relax the gluten.

7. Roll out each round of dough into an

oval shape using a rolling pin. Take one piece of rolled-out matcha dough and arrange on top of a rolled-out white dough. Run the rolling pin over the stacked dough several times so that the two begin to merge. This process is what will lovingly render the swirling, jelly roll-esque design to the loaf. Take one short end of the dough and fold just to the center of the oval, then take the other end and fold to meet the top. It should look almost like a folded letter. Flip over the dough with the folds facing down and flatten with the rolling pin. Flip dough over again so the folds facing upwards and then begin to roll the dough up. Place the rolled-up dough onto the bread pan. Repeat this process with the remaining pieces of dough.

8. Once all the rolled-up pieces of dough are arranged in the loaf pan, place cellophane or a towel over the rolls. Let them rise again (about 40-60 minutes) until each has doubled in size.

9. To create your egg wash, whisk together one egg and a tablespoon of milk or water in a small bowl. Once the dough has risen to its proper point, brush the egg wash on top and sprinkle with sesame seeds. Bake at 325°F for 30 minutes, checking halfway to ensure that the bread is not browning too fast on top. If this happens, simply tent your bread with aluminum foil.

10. Allow the bread to cool briefly, then carefully remove and set onto a wire rack. Slice gently, and you're ready to dig in! Savor its flavors and softness best while the bread is still warm

2. Gluten-Free Green Tea Bread

This recipe is developed specifically for a 2-lb breadmaker BB-PAC20 (https://www.amazon.com/Zojirushi-BB-PAC20-Virtuoso-Bread-maker-setting/dp/B0067MQM48/ref=sr_1_1?ie=UTF8&qid=1495516393&sr=8-1&keywords=2-lb.+bread+maker+bb-pac20)

Yields one standard (8½" x 4½") loaf

Ingredients:
- 1 + 1/2 cups milk
- 3 eggs, beaten
- 3 tablespoon vegetable oil
- 1 tablespoon apple cider vinegar
- 2 tablespoons honey (increase or decrease by the tablespoon as per your preference)
- 1 tablespoon matcha powder
- 1 + 1/2 cups brown rice flour
- 2 + 1/3 cups potato starch
- 1 tablespoon salt
- 1 tablespoon xanthan gum
- 1 tablespoon active dry yeast

Directions:

1. In a large bowl, use a whisk to mix together the brown rice flour, potato starch, and matcha.

2. Add in liquid ingredients (honey, vinegar, oil, eggs, milk) to the baking pan. Then, incorporate the powder mixture from Step 1, along with the xanthan gum and salt.

3. Make a small indentation in the flour using your fist or a spoon, and place the yeast there - be careful that the yeast does not touch the liquid and salt.

4. Place the baking pan in the "Home Bakery", and set it to the "Gluten Free" course.

5. Set the crust control, and press START. Once the beep has sounded, use a rubber spatula to push down any flour that may be stuck to the side. Proceed cautiously if the kneading blades are still moving.

6. Once the bread finishes baking, remove immediately and put it on a cooling rack. After it has cooled, slice and serve your bread which can be enjoyed by even the most finicky of stomachs!

3. Candied Ginger and Green Tea Bread

The ginger and lemon included in this recipe will wake up your senses, and play perfectly with the soft depth of green tea leaves. Enjoy it as a breakfast, a snack, or even better, make it an excuse for a tea party! This one goes perfectly with a bit of cream cheese and apricot preserves, a drizzle of honey, or savored with a slice of goat cheese.

Yields one 9 x 5-inch (23 x 13-cm) loaf

Ingredients:
• 2 cups all-purpose flower
• 1 teaspoon salt
• 1 tablespoon ground ginger
• 1 teaspoon baking powder
• ¼ teaspoon baking soda
• ¼ cup green tea leaves, finely ground
• ¼ cup finely chopped candied ginger

- zest of 1 lemon
- 4 eggs
- 1 cup superfine sugar
- 1 tablespoon vanilla extract
- ¾ cup virgin olive oil or vegetable oil

- 2 tablespoons lemon juice (fresh is best)

Directions:

1. Preheat oven to 350°F. Position a baking rack in the lower half of the oven. Lightly oil a 9 x 5 x 3-inch loaf pan and line the inside with parchment paper.

2. Sift the flour, salt, baking powder, ginger, and baking soda together in a bowl. Then, stir in the green tea, lemon zest, and chopped candied ginger, and set aside. If you have green tea that needs finer grinding, a spice/coffee grinder will do the trick.

3. Break the eggs into the bowl of a food processor and process for about a minute, or until light and frothy in appearance. With the motor still running, slowly add in the sugar through the feed tube in 3 stages, allowing about 30 seconds between each addition. This will ensure that it is incorporated thoroughly. Combine the oil, lemon juice, and vanilla in a small measuring cup and drizzle through the feed tube onto the egg mixture, keeping the motor running as you do so.

4. Remove the processor top and add in all of the dry ingredients (flour, ginger, baking soda, baking powder, sugar, lemon zest, salt, green tea) all at once. Pulse until the mixture is just blended, and then pour the batter into the prepared pan.

5. Bake for about 50 minutes, or until a toothpick inserted comes out clean. Remove the pan from the oven and let the cake rest for at least 30 minutes on a rack. When cool, remove bread from pan and wrap tightly in cellophane. You're now ready to enjoy!

4. Matcha Green Tea Milk Bread

This bread will stay soft and fluffy for days!

Yields: one standard (8½" x 4½") loaf

Ingredients:
- 2 + ½ cups bread flour
- 1/2 teaspoon salt
- 4 tablespoons sugar
- 1 large egg
- ½ cup milk
- 120g tangzhong (about 1/2 a cup; refer to the recipe listed previously)
- 2 tablespoons matcha powder
- 2 teaspoon instant yeast
- 3 tablespoons butter (softened) change the color of your finished product)
- 1 teaspoon baking powder
- dash salt

Directions:

1. Combine the flour, salt, sugar, and instant yeast into a bowl of a standing mixer. Using your fist or a spoon, make a well in the center. Add in all wet ingredients (butter, tangzhong, milk, and egg), and attach the dough hook onto your standing mixer and begin mixing at medium speed. Knead until your dough comes together, then add in the butter, and continue the kneading process. Knead until the dough has reached its proper consistency (discussed in the first recipe).

2. Knead the dough into a ball shape, and split in half. Put half of the dough back into the mixer. Add in the matcha powder and continue kneading for

about 2 minutes at medium speed or until the matcha powder is thoroughly mixed into the dough. Take 2 large bowls and grease them with oil. Place each dough ball into a greased bowl and cover with cellophane or a dampened towel. Let it proof until it's doubled in size, about 40 minutes.

3. Transfer the proofed dough to a clean surface and divide each dough into four equal portions. Knead into balls, cover with cellophane, and let rest for an additional 15 minutes.

4. Roll out each portion of the dough into an oval shape using a rolling pin. Take one piece of matcha dough, rolled out into an oval, and put it on top of the white dough also rolled out into an oval. Run the rolling pin a few times on top so that the two doughs begin to stick together and merge into one piece of dough. Take one end of the dough and fold to meet the middle of the oval. Take the other end and fold it to meet on top.

5. Flip the dough over with folds face down, and flatten it using a rolling pin.

6. Flip the dough over with folds facing up. Now, roll the dough up. Place each of the rolls into the bread pan and cover the rolls with cellophane. Let them rise until double the size, approximately 40 more minutes.

7. Brush egg mixture on top to create that shiny, desirable egg wash finish.

8. Bake at 325 degrees F for approximately 30 minutes. Take it out, and you're ready to go!

5. Vegan Gluten-Free Matcha Banana Bread With Pistachios

A homey classic gets a contemporary twist in this gluten-free dish!

Yields one loaf

Ingredients:
- 2 ripe bananas
- 1 1/4 cup gluten free flour blend (if your flour blend doesn't have xanthan gum included, add 1 teaspoon of xanthan gum.)
- 3/4 cup almond flour
- 2 vegan eggs
- 1/2 cup finely chopped pistachios (finely chopped almonds will also work)
- 1 teaspoon vanilla
- 3/4 cup almond milk
- 3 tablespoons sweetened matcha powder (if your matcha is unsweetened, add 3 tablespoons of sugar to the recipe)
- 1/2 cup melted coconut oil
- 3/4 cup sugar (brown is fine, but will change the color of your finished product)
- 1 teaspoon baking powder
- dash salt

Directions:

1. Preheat the oven to 350 degrees.

2. Spray coconut oil into a bread loaf pan.

3. In a mixer, add in the coconut oil, almond milk, vanilla, and bananas.

4. Turn the mixer on slow.

5. Slowly incorporate dry ingredients (sugar, salt, baking powder, matcha, flour, and pistachios) a little at a time.

6. Once the dry ingredients are mixed, up the speed to medium for 1 minute.

7. Pour the batter into the loaf pan and bake 25-30 minutes until done. This bread is great enjoyed alone, or with a dollop of any (dairy, or dairy-free) vanilla ice-cream. For extra flair, top with an additional helping of chopped nuts or sliced banana.

6. Matcha Chocolate Swirl Bread

If you haven't had this combination of green tea and chocolate yet... you've been missing out.
Yields two 9 x 5 inch loaves

- To make the matcha bread:
- 2 + ½ cups bread flour
- 4 tablespoons sugar
- 1 large egg
- ½ cup milk
- 120g tangzhong (roughly a half cup; refer to recipe listed previously)
- 2 teaspoons instant yeast
- 3 tablespoons butter (softened)
- 1 teaspoon salt
- 2 tablespoons matcha powder

Directions

1. Combine the flour, sugar, salt, matcha, and instant yeast in a bowl of a standing mixer. Use your fist or a spoon to create a well in the center, and add in all of the wet (milk, egg, tangzhong, butter) ingredients. Fit the dough hook attachment onto your standing mixer and begin mixing at medium speed, kneading until your dough comes together, then add in the butter and continue kneading until dough reaches its proper consistency.

2. Knead the dough into a ball shape. Take a large bowl and grease with oil. Place dough into greased bowl and cover with cellophane or a damp towel. Let it proof until it's doubled in size, for about 40 minutes.

3. Now, it's time to make the chocolate dough! Combine the flour, salt, cocoa powder, sugar, and instant yeast in a bowl of a standing mixer. Form a well in the center. Add in all wet ingredients (the same as mentioned previously).

4. Follow the same directions listed in Steps 1 and 2 to create and knead the dough.

5. To swirl your two infused doughs together for baking, follow the same steps for rolling and baking as shown in the first recipe. Bon appétit!

7. Matcha Croissants

This might be the most addictive one yet-- as if croissants weren't already addictive enough!
Yields 24 croissants
 Ingredients:

- 3 tablespoons unsalted butter
- 24 tablespoons (3 sticks) cold unsalted European-style-butter.• 1 + 3/4 cups milk
- 2 teaspoons kosher salt
- 4 teaspoons instant yeast
- 4 + 1/4 cups all-purpose flour
- 4 tablespoons matcha powder
- 1/4 cup sugar
- 1 large egg
- 1 teaspoon cold water
- black sesame seeds
- fi ling of your choice (red bean paste, chocolate peanut butter, hazelnut spread, bite-size candy bars...experiment!
- icing sugar or honey (your preference)

Directions:

1. Melt three tablespoons of classic, unsalted butter in a saucepan over low heat. Remove from heat and immediately stir in the milk. Whisk in yeast. Transfer milk mixture to the bowl of a standing mixer. Add in flour, matcha powder, salt, and sugar. Using a dough hook, knead on low speed until a proper dough forms for about 2 to 3 minutes. Increase speed to medium-low and knead for one more minute. Remove bowl from the mixer and cover with cellophane. Let dough rest at room temperature for 30 minutes.

2. Transfer the dough to a parchment paper-lined baking sheet and shape into a rectangle about 10 by 7-inches, 1 inch thick. Secure with plastic and refrigerate for 2 hours.

3.While dough chills, fold the 24-inch length of parchment in half to create a

12-inch rectangle. Fold over three open sides of the rectangle to form an 8-inch square with enclosed sides. Crease the folds firmly. Place 24 tablespoons of cold butter directly on the counter and beat with rolling pin for about 60 seconds, until the butter is just pliable but not warm, then fold butter in on itself using a bench scraper. Beat into a 6-inch square. Unfold the parchment envelope. Using a bench scraper, transfer butter to the center of parchment, refolding at creases to enclose. Turn packet over so that flaps are underneath and gently roll until the butter fills the parchment square, paying attention to even thickness. Refrigerate for at least 45 minutes.

4. Put the dough in the freezer. After about 30 minutes, transfer the dough to a lightly floured counter and roll into a 17 by 8-inch rectangle with long sides running parallel to the edge of the counter. Unwrap butter and place in the center of the dough. Fold sides of dough over the cylinder of butter so that they meet in the center. Press seam together using fingertips. With rolling pin, press firmly on each open end of the packet. Roll out lengthwise into 24 by 8-inch rectangle. Starting at the bottom of the dough, fold into thirds (like a letter shape) into an 8-inch square. Place dough 90 degrees anti-clockwise. Roll out again into 24 by 8-inch rectangle and fold into three. Place dough on a sheet and wrap tightly with plastic. Return to the freezer for another 30 minutes.

5. Transfer dough again to a lightly floured counter, so that top flap opens on the right. Roll out dough lengthwise into 24 by 8-inch rectangle and fold into thirds. Place dough on sheet, wrap tightly with plastic and refrigerate for 2 hours.

6. Transfer dough to the freezer. After 30 minutes, transfer to a lightly floured counter and roll into 18 by 16-inch

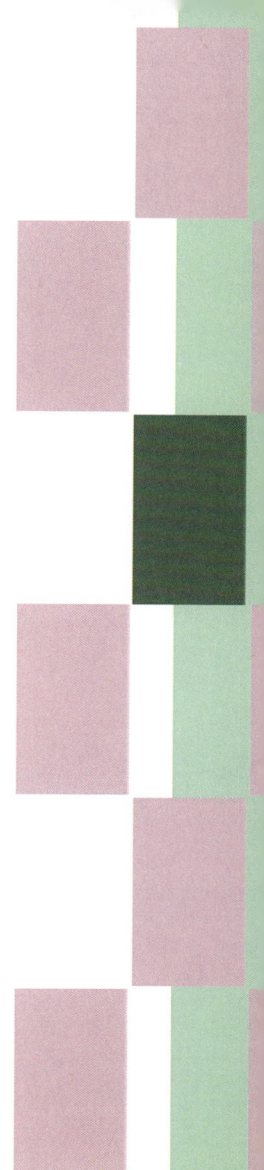

rectangle with the long side of the rectangle parallel to edge of the counter. Fold the upper half of dough over the lower half. Using a ruler, mark the dough at 3-inch intervals along the bottom edge with a bench scraper (you should have five marks). Move ruler to the top edge of the dough, measuring in 1 1/2 inches from left, then use this mark to measure out 3-inch intervals (you should have six marks). Beginning at the lower left corner, use a knife to cut dough connecting the marks. You will have 12 triangles and five diamonds. Unfold the diamonds and cut into ten triangles

7. Position one triangle on the counter, while keeping remaining triangles covered with plastic. Cut a 1/2-inch slit in the center of the short side of the triangle. Place a dollop of whatever optional filling you decided to use in the center of the bottom of the short side. Grasp triangle by two corners on either side of the slit and stretch gently, then stretch the bottom point. Place a triangle on the counter so that the point is facing you. Fold down both sides of the slit. Roll the top of triangle partway toward the point. Carefully hold point with one hand and stretch again. Resume rolling, tucking the point underneath. Curve ends gently toward each other, so they create a crescent. Repeat with remaining triangles.

8. Place 12 croissants on two parchment-lined sheets at least 2 and a half inches apart and wrap with plastic. Let it rise at room temperature until it is almost double in size, between 2 and 3 hours. Preheat the oven to 425 degrees. Whisk together egg, water, and a dash of salt in a small bowl. Brush croissants with the egg wash. Sprinkle with black sesame seeds.

9. Place the croissants in the oven and reduce the temperature to 400 degrees. Bake for 12 minutes, then switch and rotate baking sheets. Continue to bake until it becomes deep golden brown. Transfer to wire rack and cool about 15 minutes. Dust with matcha powder and icing sugar/ honey if desired. Serve warm or at room temperature.

8. Vanilla Matcha Bread

This treat is pretty healthy, but you'll be surprised by its lightly decadent bite. For extra decadence, try topping with a bit of raspberry preservative.
Sliced vanilla match bread is about 12 servings.

Ingredients:
- 1/2 cup oat flour
- 2 teaspoons baking powder
- 2 scoops vanilla protein powder
- 1/8 cup matcha powder
- 2 eggs
- 1/4 butter
- 4 tablespoons honey
- 1 large, ripe banana
- 3 teaspoons vanilla extract

1. Preheat oven to 400 F. Line a medium loaf pan with parchment or foil, grease, and set aside.

2. Pour your oats into a blender and pulse until the oats have been ground into a flour-like texture. Pour into a large mixing bowl, then mix in your vanilla protein powder, baking powder, and matcha powder. Set mixture aside.

3. Next, melt your butter and pour it into the blender along with the other wet ingredients-- vanilla extract, honey, and banana. Blend until combined, then pour into the mixing bowl of dry ingredients. Mix until well incorporated, then pour into your greased loaf pan.

4. Bake on the middle rack of the oven for 30-35 minutes. To check if it's ready, do the toothpick test.

5. Leave to cool, then slice up and enjoy! It can stay up to a week.

9. Matcha Melon Bread

Melon bread is a classic sweet bun. it hails from Japan. In this recipe, a ball of fluffy matcha bread is coated in sweet matcha cookie dough!
It yields six servings

To make the bread dough:
- 1 tablespoon matcha powder
- 1 + ¾ cup flour (bread or all purpose both work)
- 2 teaspoons dry yeast
- 1/4 cup sugar
- 1 + ¾ tablespoons butter
- 3/4 cup of eggs, beaten
- 1/2 cup milk
- Dash of salt

To make the cookie dough:
- 3/4 cup flour (cake or all purpose both work)
- 2 tablespoons matcha powder
- 1/2 tablespoon baking powder
- 4 + ¼ tablespoon butter
- 1/3 cup sugar
- 1 egg yolk
- Milk as needed

Directions:

1. Sift the flour and matcha for the bread component together in a bowl.

2. Evenly add the salt, sugar, yeast, butter, egg, and milk, and mix well. Knead by hand until the dough begins to come together and is smooth.

3. Form the dough into a ball, return it to the bowl, cover with cellophane, and leave in a warm place for about an hour to allow for rising.

4. When the dough is double in size, remove it from the bowl and knead out any air bubbles that may have formed. Separate into six separate pieces, shape into balls, and cover with cellophane or a damp towel. Allow the dough rounds to expand again, to about 1.5 times their size.

5. to make the cookie dough, sift the

remaining matcha, flour, and baking powder together. Place the butter in a bowl and allow the ingredients to come to room temperature.

6. Mix the butter until it takes on a creamy texture. Add some of the sugar (about 1/3) cups) to the butter and mix until well incorporated. Repeat 3-4 times until all of the sugar is mixed in and it looks white and smooth. Mix in the milk and egg yolk. Add the sugar and butter little by little, mixing well.

7. Fold the dry ingredients (flour, mat-cha, baking powder, remaining sugar) into the wet ingredients (butter, milk, and egg). Once the dough fully comes together, roll and form into a cylinder shape, and wrap it in cellophane.

8. Put in the fridge and allow to cool.

9. Remove the cookie dough from the refrigerator, roll out, and cut it into six sheets. Pre-heat the oven to 325 F.

10. Place each ball of bread dough onto a cookie sheet, leaving sufficient space in between each piece. Lightly press down on the dough to somewhat flatten it.

11. Lay a piece of cookie dough on each mound of bread dough. Using a knife, lightly make a crosshatch pattern in the

10. Green Tea Banana Coconut Bread With Black Sesame Seed

This one will be so pretty that you won't want to eat it! (Except, that you should, because it's chockful of all the best flavors.)
Yields one standard (8½" x 4½") loaf

Ingredients:
- 3 ripe bananas
- 1 cup raw turbinado sugar
- 2 teaspoons vanilla extract
- 2 tablespoons butter, melted at room temperature
- 1/2 cup coconut milk
- 2 eggs
- 1 3/4 cups flour
- 4 teaspoons matcha powder
- 1/4 teaspoon salt
- 1 teaspoon baking soda
- 3 tablespoons black sesame seeds
- Optional: coconut flakes, turbinado sugar, or banana slices for topping

Directions:

1. Pre-heat the oven to about 350 degrees and grease one loaf pan.

2. In a large bowl, mash the bananas to your preference.

3. Stir in the sugar and vanilla extract.

4. Add the eggs and stir until thoroughly incorporated.

5. Ensure the melted butter has cooled, then stir in the butter and coconut milk.

6. Add the matcha powder, salt, baking soda, flour, and sesame seeds and gently stir the mixture until combined.

7. Pour the mixture into the loaf pan and top with coconut, banana, sugar, and black sesame seeds.

8. Bake for 50-60 minutes or until a knife comes out clean. Cool completely before cutting into the loaf. It's ready to enjoy!

What you should know about using green tea for cake making

TIPS AND TRICKS WHEN USING GREEN TEA FOR BAKING CAKES

Are you looking to infuse your cakes with green tea but don't know where to begin? Then you've come to the right place. Green tea is an excellent, all-natural herb that can be used in a variety of different ways. Adding it to your cake will create a robust taste that is unforgettable. It also adds a healthier edge to your cake, providing you with many anti-oxidants and other healthy items. Here's what you need to know about this process before trying it out on your own.

Trying Both Loose-Leaf Tea and Matcha

Before you start baking cakes with green tea, it is important to understand that there are two different kinds you can use. When most people think of green tea, they think of the loose-leaf tea that can be boiled and served as a drink. While you can use this type of tea in your cake baking, you should typically use matcha when baking your cakes.

What is matcha? It is a powder of green tea leaves grown in a unique way. They are sheltered from sunlight and, as a result, become greener than regular green tea leaves. As a result, matcha has a different color, texture, and taste when used in baking. Try experimenting with both loose-leaf tea and matcha to see which you prefer.

Throughout this article, assume that you're going to be using matcha rather than loose-leaf green tea. Why? Because matcha creates less residue and is simply easier to use when

baking. There are a few advantages to using loose-leaf green tea, but use matcha until you're comfortable with this baking method.

Getting the Tea In Your Cake

There are several different ways that you can get matcha green tea into your cake and each has its advantages and disadvantages. We are going to break these methods down to give you an insight into each. Any one of them will work to infuse your cake with matcha green tea, but you may prefer the taste generated using a specific method.

Dropping the Tea Directly In the Batter

The easiest way to get green tea into your cakes is to grind it up and drop it in your batter. You can use this method with either loose-leaf tea or matcha. The benefit to this approach is that it doesn't take much work. The major downside is that it is the less efficient. While your cake will have some green tea flavor, it won't be as potent. However, for those who want just a hint of green tea in their cakes, this method is the best. To increase its potency, use matcha instead of loose-leaf green tea. This will give it more of a kick.

Steeping the Cake's Batter

The next method of getting green tea into your cake is by steeping some matcha powder in milk. Let your green tea steep in your milk for an appropriate amount of time; we suggest about 10-15 minutes for the most effectiveness. Pull out the tea infuser after it is finished, remove any excess powder or floating leaves, and bake your cake with this milk. It will create a very rich and delicious flavor without overpowering the rest of your cake mix.

The other benefit of this method is a stronger green tea taste and a lack of green tea residue in the cake. This residue is particularly decreased if you used matcha instead of loose-leaf green tea. The downside of this approach is that it can't be used by those making vegan or lactose-free cakes.

Create Tea-Infused Butter

While the methods mentioned above work reasonably well, you need to create tea-infused butter to maximize your cake's green tea flavoring. Take the appropriate amount of unsalted butter, place it in a pan, melt it slowly, and add a teaspoon or two of green tea. Use matcha powder to infuse it the most efficiently. Mix it in as the butter melts to spread it slowly throughout.

The benefit here is that the green tea will be infused directly into the grain of your cake. As a result, you'll get the most potent green tea taste possible. However, this method takes some time to implement and will leave small bits of green tea in your cake. This is another benefit of using matcha instead of loose-leaf green tea. You simply won't have as much residue.

Try Out

Different Flour Types for Unique Results

Another fun way you can experiment with your green tea cake is to try different types of flour. If you're going gluten-free, coconut or even almond flour are an excellent choice. Even if you're not limiting your gluten intake, these flour types add a slightly different flavor to your cake that can pair well with green tea.

Almond flour in particular works well in cake infused with green tea. Both have a rather earthy flavor that tastes good when mixed. You can then add a coconut dusting to the top when it is done to create a delicious and unique cake.

Some Final Thoughts

As you can see, there are several inter-esting ways that you can use green tea when baking cakes. Infusing it requires some careful preparation, planning, and experimentation, but when you're done, you will have a unique and potent flavoring that will make your cake delicious to a wide range of people.

If you're interested in infusing green tea in your cake frosting, try using matcha for the best effect. Its potency and its green coloring make it a fascinating addition to any cake. For some, it may be a little too rich, but it will be perfect for those who love their green tea strong.

13 10 Yummy Green Tea Cake Recipes

If you enjoy green tea you might already be aware that it can be used in baking and other dishes. It isn't only a beverage. You can use both loose leaf green tea and matcha tea powder in various recipes.

The loose-leaf variety is generally what we think of in terms of green tea. Matcha is a finely milled green tea that is sourced from ground tencha leaves. The green tea that comes from Gyokuro is the one that is made from tencha. That is what is used to make matcha powder.

When cooking with green tea, experienced chefs and home cooks will use the loose-leaf tea to infuse a smoky or steamed flavor into dishes. Matcha green tea powder is ideal for use in baking, as you will see in the following recipes.

1 - Green Tea Cake

Ingredients:
- 3 Eggs
- 1/2 Cup of fine sugar
- 1/2 Cup of grape seed oil
- 3/4 Cup of plain yogurt
- 1 tsp of vanilla extract
- 1 1/2 Cups all purpose flour
- 1 tsp of baking powder
- 6 tsps of matcha tea powder

Directions:

1. Preheat the oven to 350°F.

2. In a large mixing bowl, beat or whisk the eggs, sugar, vanilla, and oil together until fluffy, then stir in the yogurt.

3. In another large bowl, sift the flour, baking powder, and matcha powder together.

4. Using a rubber spatula, gently fold the flour mixture into the wet ingredients until well combined but not mixed too much.

5. Pour the cake batter into a greased cake pan evenly and bake for 35 minutes or until the top becomes golden brown and a toothpick comes out clean from the center.

2 - Matcha Mint Cookies and Cream Napoleon

Ingredients:
- 1 Cup heavy cream for whipping
- 1 or 2 Drops of mint flavoring extract
- 2 tsps matcha tea powder
- 12 Chocolate wafer cookies

Directions:

1. Beat the heavy cream until stiff peaks form. Gently mix in the matcha powder and mint extract.

2. On a plate, lay down a wafer and spoon 2 tsps. of whipped cream on top. Add another wafer and continue layering with the cream and wafers until you have 6 layers. Repeat on another plate. If you have any whipped cream left, cover the cakes completely.

3. Place the cakes in the refrigerator for 12 to 24 hours. The wafers will

3 - Pound Cake with Green Tea Powder

Ingredients:
- 2 Large eggs
- 1/4 Cup butter
- 1 Cup fine sugar
- 1/2 Cup milk
- 1/2 tsp pure vanilla extract
- 1 Cup all purpose flour
- 1 TBSP matcha tea powder
- 1 tsp baking powder
- 1/4 tsp sea salt

Directions:

1. Preheat the oven to 325°F.

2. Using a hand mixer, cream the butter and sugar together. Add the eggs, milk, and vanilla extract. Hand mix until well combined.

3. In a separate bowl, combine the flour, matcha powder, baking powder, and sea salt using a wooden spoon or whisk. Then, add the wet ingredients and blend until smooth.

4. Generously oil or butter a bread loaf pan with and pour the batter into it. Bake for up to 50 minutes until golden brown. Test the center with a toothpick to see if it comes out clean.

4 - Matcha Icing for Cakes

Ingredients:
- 3 TBS butter, melted
- 1 TBS honey
- 1 TBS pure vanilla extract
- 1 TBS matcha tea powder
- 1 Cup confectioner's sugar

Directions:

Whisk together all ingredients until

smooth and pour over warm cakes,

brownies, or cheesecake to glaze

them.

5 - Matcha Mochi Cakes

Ingredients:
- 15 ounce can of coconut milk
- 1 cup water
- 1 tsp pure vanilla extract
- 2 cups sugar
- 1 teaspoon baking powder
- (1) 16-ounce box mochiko rice flour
- 2 TBS matcha powder

Directions:

1. Preheat the oven to 350°F.

2. In a large bowl, combine coconut milk, water, vanilla, and sugar. Mix with a hand mixer until sugar is mostly dissolved.

3. Slowly add baking powder and flour and continue to mix until the batter thickens. Then, add the matcha powder and mix well.

4. Spray or oil the inside of a 9" by 13" glass baking dish and pour the cake batter into the dish. Bake the mochi batter for 60 minutes.

5. Allow to cool to room temperature. Cut into squares and serve immediately. You can drizzle maple syrup on top.

6 - Cheesecake Infused with Green Tea Powder (Matcha)

Ingredients:
- 16 ounces of cream cheese at room temperature
- 3/4 Cup sugar
- 2 Eggs at room temperature
- 2 tsps pure vanilla extract
- 1 TBS green tea powder
- 1 Pre-packaged graham cracker crust

Directions:

1. Preheat the oven to 350°F.

2. Using a standing mixer, cream together the softened cheese and sugar. Add the eggs, vanilla extract, and tea powder.

Mix al of this well.

3. Pour the wet mixture into the prepared graham cracker pie crust. Bake for 25 minutes, then refrigerate until chilled

7 - Easy Chocolate Cake Dusted with Matcha

Ingredients:
- 1 box of devil's food chocolate cake mix
- Water, oil, and eggs as recipe requires
- 1 TBS matcha powder for dusting

Directions:

1. Preheat the oven to 350°F

2. Prepare the cake mix as directed on the box and pour the batter into a greased 9" baking pan; bake as directed

3. After the cake has cooled, dust it with matcha powder and cut into pieces

8 - Raw Green Tea Leaf Breakfast Cakes

Ingredients:

- A handful of fresh spinach leaves
- 2 tsps. dried & crushed green tea leaves
- 1 ripe banana
- 1 cup almond milk
- 1 tbs. honey
- 3 tsps. fresh lemon juice
- 1/2 tsp. pure vanilla extract
- 1 Cup water
- 2/3 tsp. agar-agar flakes

Directions:

1. Combine first ingredients in a food processor, blend until creamy, and set aside

2. In a sauce pan, heat the water and the agar-agar on low

3. Whisk this mixture until it just begins to thicken, remove it from the heat, and continue whisking for another 30 seconds

4. Combine the agar-agar mixture with the other ingredients and pour into a baking dish

5. Place the dish in the refrigerator for approximately 45 minutes until the cake has set

6. Cut into squares and serve with any topping of fruits or nuts

9 - Matcha Shortbread Cakes

Ingredients:
- 1 3/4 cups all-purpose flour
- 3/4 cup confectioner's sugar
- 1 1/2 tbs. matcha green tea powder
- 10 tbs. butter at room temperature
- 3 egg yolks at room temperature
- 1 cup granulated sugar

Directions:

1. In a standing mixer with the paddle attachment on, cream the confectioner's sugar, matcha powder, and butter

2. Add the flour and stir until just combined; then, mix in the egg yolks until the dough comes together

3. Mold the dough into a ball, then flatten it to a round disc shape; wrap this in plastic and refrigerate for at least 30 minutes

4. Preheat the oven to 350°F

5. With a rolling pin, flatten the cold dough to about 1/2" thick

6. Slice the dough into 2" squares or use a glass to cut into circles and coat all over with the sugar. Place the small cakes on a sheet pan and bake for approximately 14 minutes (these will resemble cakey cookies when cooled)

10 - Afternoon Tea Cakes

Ingredients:
- 8 eggs
- 12 egg yolks
- 2 cups sugar
- 1 1/3 cups cake flour
- 1/2 cup cornstarch
- 1/4 cup matcha tea powder
- 8 egg whites
- 1/2 tsp. cream of tartar
- 1/2 cup sugar
- Confectioner's sugar to sprinkle on top

Directions:

1. Preheat oven to 350°F

2. In a large bowl, beat together whole eggs, yolks, and 2 cups of sugar for about 5 minutes

3. In another bowl, sift the dry ingredients together, then fold them into the wet mixture

4. In a standing mixer, whip the egg whites and cream of tartar until foamy; add 1/2 cup sugar and beat until stiff peaks form, then gently fold this mixture into the batter

5. Grease a large sheet pan, line it with parchment paper, and spread the batter on the paper evenly

6. Bake the large cake for 12 minutes or until the edges just start to brown

7. Turn over onto a counter or cutting board and remove the parchment paper; when cooled, sprinkle with confectioner's sugar and cut into 2" squares

Green tea leaves and powder, otherwise known as matcha, are great in baked goods, especially cakes. Matcha imparts a mild green tea flavor and gives baked goods a distinctive green hue. Be mindful that green tea and matcha have caffeine in them when cooking or baking.

ABOUT THE AUTHOR

Kei Nishida is a Japanese green tea enthusiast, a writer, and the founder and CEO of Japanese Green Tea Company. His passion for introducing America to the tea of his homeland was the catalyst for creating the only company that brings high-quality tea from Arahataen Green Tea Farms to the rest of the world.

Having spent his early years in Japan, Kei Nishida has been fervent about green tea throughout his life. He credits his first career as a software engineer at Hewlett Packard (HP) for his interest in science, research, and writing that influences his drive to source the best green tea for a wider audience today. He is also drawn to the research-driven approach by Arahataen farm to utilize the best technology for every batch.

Today, you can find his published work in Fresh Cup Magazine, Yoga Digest Magazine, T-Ching and more. He is also the author of three published books: I will Teach You How to Be Healthy By Using Japanese Green Tea, Green Tea Mania: 250+ Green Tea Facts, Cooking and Brewing Tips & Trivia You (Probably) Didn't Know, and Green Tea Cha - How Japan and the World Enjoy Green Tea in the 21st Century.

KEI NISHIDA'S
BOOKS

I WILL TEACH YOU HOW TO BE HEALTHY BY DRINKING USING JAPANESE GREEN TEA

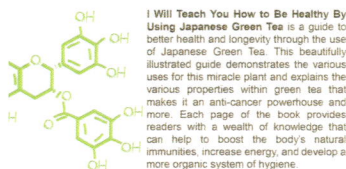

Paperback: 120 pages
Language: English
ISBN-10: 1544093322
ISBN-13: 978-1544093321
Product Dimensions: 8.2" x 0.3" x 6"
Shipping Weight: 7.8 ounces

I Will Teach You How to Be Healthy By Using Japanese Green Tea is a guide to better health and longevity through the use of Japanese Green Tea. This beautifully illustrated guide demonstrates the various uses for this miracle plant and explains the various properties within green tea that makes it an anti-cancer power-house and more. Each page of the book provides readers with a wealth of knowledge that can help to boost the body's natural immunities, increase energy, and develop a more organic system of hygiene.

Everything you wanted to know about Japanese Green Tea can be found within the pages of Kei Nishida's amazing new book. Educational and entertaining, I Will Teach You How to Be Healthy By Using Japanese Green Tea is the perfect book from which to launch a healthier more robust lifestyle. Readers will learn everything from how to brew it properly to making aromatherapy oils from its leaves. It's not just a book about tea, it's a book about living better.

GREEN TEA MANIA : 250+ GREEN TEA FACTS, COOKING AND BREWING TIPS & TRIVIA YOU (PROBABLY) DIDN'T KNOW

Paperback: 120 pages
Language: English
ISBN-10: 1544093322
ISBN-13: 978-1544093321
Product Dimensions: 8.2 x
0.3 x 6 inches
Shipping Weight: 7.8 ounces

Green Tea Mania is a must have book for trivia lovers and fans of green tea. This is author Kei Nishida's second book on green tea following up his earlier work, I Will Teach You to Be Healthy Using Japanese Green Tea. Green Tea Mania delivers 200+ facts and an array of delightful pictures in its 120 pages. This full color trivia tome helps paint a picture on not only the health properties of this magical leaf, but also its history and cultivation. Did you know that Black Tea, Oolong Tea, and Green Tea come from the same plant or that their labels really just describe where the leaf was left off in the fermentation process? Learn about the unusual uses for Green tea such as "Green Tea Beer" or cake. Find out how to get more of the antioxidant Catechin out of tea by adding one simple ingredient. These facts and hundreds more are all contained inside this beautiful guide to Green Tea.

This book is a must-have for the health conscious or Green Tea enthusiast.

GREEN TEA CHA : HOW JAPAN AND THE WORLD ENJOY GREEN TEA IN THE 21ST CENTURY

GREEN TEA CHA

How Japan and the World

Enjoy Green Tea in the 21st Century

Paperback: 152 pages
Language: English
ISBN-10: 1546704418
ISBN-13: 978-1546704416
Product Dimensions: 5.5 x
0.4 x 8.5 inches
Shipping Weight: 9 ounces

Kei Nishida is back with his latest book on the subject of Green Tea, Green Tea Cha, How Japan and the world Enjoys Green Tea in the 21st Century. In this 143 page book Tokyo native Nishida covers the changing use and appreciation for tea in the 21st Century. He brings together a collection of facts and observances that allows the reader to peer into the cultural mindset of those who enjoy Green Tea. He begins by explaining how tea is enjoyed in Japan today and the merger of traditional Japanese culture with that of the jihanki (vending machines) and ends with a discussion of Green Tea Beverages that "you've never heard of before but are drop dead delicious."

Each chapter brings together a plethora of information about the uses of Green Tea in his pleasant, informative style, encouraging the reader to seek out these drinks and dishes for themselves. By the end of the book readers will not only have a list of "must try" drinks and dishes but also an appreciation for this powerful, tasty antioxidant.

Join Green Tea Club

Did you enjoy the book?

Get more recipes, articles and video by Kei Nishida by joining Green Tea Club.

Sign up free to Green Tea Club to get tips and exclusive articles by Kei Nishida about how to use your matcha and green tea for a healthy lifestyle.

You also get immediate access to 10% Off coupon at Japanese Green Tea Company for your first order. Unsubscribe anytime.

Join Now Free at: https://www.japanesegreenteain.com/GreenTeaClub

www.ingramcontent.com/pod-product-compliance
Lightning Source LLC
Chambersburg PA
CBRC100736150426
42811CB00070B/1913